On Being the Being

Also by the author

Poetry
Steel Umbrellas

On Being
the Being

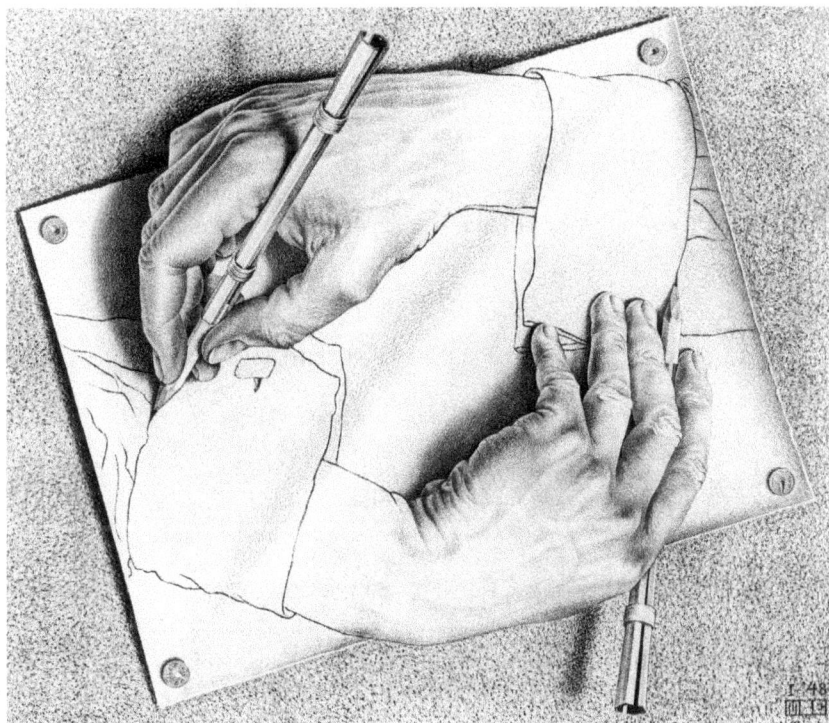

An analysis on the establishment of Being and the non-existent-self

David Sutherland

Archer Books

Published in 2012 in the United States by
Archer Books
P. O. Box 1254
Santa Maria, CA 93456
www.archer-books.com —jtcimag@archer-books.com

First Edition

Printed in the United States

Cover design: JTC Imagineering

Cover image: "Drawing Hands" by M.C. Escher
Used by permission
© The M.C. Escher Company

Paperback ISBN: 978-1-931122-25-2

Library of Congress Cataloging-in-Publication Data

Sutherland, David Hunter, 1962-
  On being the being : an analysis on the establishment of being and the non-existent self / David Sutherland. -- 1st ed.
    p. cm.
  Includes bibliographical references and index.
  ISBN 978-1-931122-21-4 (alk. paper)
  1. Self--Religious aspects. 2. Theological anthropology. 3. Ontology. I. Title.
  BL65.S38S88 2012
  126--dc23
                          2012018182

In memory of Alan Watts

Preface

Humanity; man, woman and child have struggled to understand the mystery of who and what we are in this strange, beautiful and often bizarre world we call home. Our struggle as conscious beings has heralded some of our brightest achievements in the fields of the arts, sciences and philosophies. Unfortunately, it has also been the root cause of some of our darkest moments in history committed against each other in our wars and atrocities. In this respect, we can say that the most dangerous aspect of what we are, is in the not knowing who we are. In this book we will approach a subject often seen as taboo at the risk of discovering for ourselves who this strange, noble and often paradoxical being is, you. We will investigate the cultural mores of society in order to begin to understand from a psychological and intellectual perspective what has created some of our ingrained beliefs. We can then piece together a new paradigm of understanding as chapter two and three takes us on a no holds barred look at where we are and what we have discovered. In later sections of this book some of the concepts and terms used throughout history such as; soul, spirit and reality, we will investigate under this new perception of self. Finally and as the subtitle of this book suggests, we must begin our journey of being and self as it relates to our highest aspirations and dreams.

Science, philosophy and religion have played and continue to play a dominant role in shaping our world-view and perceptions. In our search for further understanding, we must build on the foundation of a number of great thinkers and sages throughout the ages. To name a few, scientists such as Niels Bohr, Julian Jaynes, Albert Einstein, Stephen Hawking and many others, can aid us in understanding the physical world we live in. Modern and past thinkers such as Daniel C. Dennett, Alan Watts, Carl Jung, John-Paul Sartre, Viktor Frankl and others, can shed light on how we come to perceive our species from a psychological perspective. Our quest for understanding would in no way be complete if we did not look upon the brilliant work of our past sages and religious icons we have come to admire. Those including Jesus of Nazareth, Shakyamuni Siddhārtha Gautama (Buddha), Abu al-Qasim Muhammad, Lao Tzu and too many others to list, can provide us the vision we need to take us on this journey. Finally, modern writers such as Wayne W. Dyer, Deepak Chopra, Kathleen Singh, Elisabeth Kubler-Ross and others can share with us their wisdom toward a reinterpretation of self. As a final note, we must proceed on this journey empty-handed and leave behind any preconceptions that can create obstacles to new discoveries and understandings. Better said by Joseph Chilton Pearce's in his book The Crack in the Cosmic Egg:

"There is a relationship between what we think is out there in the world and what we experience as being out there. There is a way in which the energy of thought and the energy of matter modify each other and interrelate. A kind of rough mirroring takes place between our mind and our reality."[1] [1]

If Mr. Pearce's statement holds any validity, then it would certainly explain the many domestic and international problems we face in a world reflecting our inner conflicts and diverse beliefs. The question of what and who we are needs answering! Let us attempt to polish this rough mirror as described by Mr. Pearce in our search for understanding.

---

1   Joseph Chilton Pearce, *The Crack In The Cosmic Egg*, (New York: Pocket Books, 1983), Chapter 1 "Circles and Lines."

1

The Split

"In the faces of men and women I see God."
—Walt Whitman

As a child or during your formative years the thought might have crossed your mind that maybe just maybe I am it, the big cheese! His or her royal Kahuna, God. Further, you might have felt at one time or another that this world with its myriad of problems, wonders and mysteries might have, by design been created for you. Well, you were never closer to the truth! Allow me to extend my hand to you in the sincerest recognition. Yes, you are God! But Whoa . . . hold on a minute, you might be asking yourself right about now whether this author has spent a little too much time in the sun, tided one too many over at the local pub or is a bit confused. Well, I am not, and I would like to take the time to show you what a magnificent, intricate and beautiful *being* you are. Nevertheless, before we begin this journey of self-discovery, if this subject matter strikes you as irreverent, or run hard against the grain of your current beliefs, please put this book down now.

Glad to see that you are still here! Let me begin by saying that it is no mere coincidence that you have found this book, for in reality you are its author! Whether you remember this is not important. You have always known the innate nature of your true *being* and the tremendous power, wisdom and knowledge you possess. This book simply represents a personal post-it note written by you as a reminder. Further, we can say that it has taken a mind staggering number of coordinated events through time, space and other means for this moment to occur. We can call this a synchronicity of sorts, or as better quoted in the words of the renowned psychoanalyst Carl Jung:

> "What I found were 'coincidences' which were connected so meaningfully that their 'chance' concurrence would represent a degree of improbability that would have to be expressed by an astronomical figure."[1]

Whatever the coincidences were or events that have occurred to lay the groundwork for you to take this journey no longer matters, you have arrived! I would further venture to guess that there have been many innate beliefs that seemed natural and obvious to you at different times in your life. The question of what if I am god? May have as quickly faded from your mind the moment it occurred. Similar to most of us, the modern world with its myriad of beliefs, rules and daily demands clamored for your attention and likely obscured these thoughts and feelings.

What are these beliefs? Well, they generally fall into the category of god, country and family and not necessarily in that order. These three categories of beliefs currently form the basis of your worldview. Let us begin with the current belief you might have about god. The dictionary defines god as the supreme divinity of the world's major religions including Judaism, Christianity and Islam. Many people believe that a super *being* exists that has created all, knows all, does all and in general has been around forever. There are many arguments for the existence of a god as well as many modern new age definitions of what a god is. Some of these new age beliefs describe god in terms of energy or nature. Additionally, it is more than

---

1. Carl G. Jung, *Synchronicity: An Acausal Connecting Principle,* (London: Routledge and Kegan Paul, 1952), Vol. 8.

likely you belong to a belief system that focused on the religions of Christianity, Islam, Judaism or an Eastern philosophy.

The question we must now ask is whether the religion or belief system you are a member of is an outcome of your birthplace and culture. To put it another way, let us say you were born and raised in Pakistan or Israel, would your world-view and belief system be that of a Muslim or a Jew? I would venture to guess it would be one of these two religions. What is puzzling with this conclusion is that any reasonable individual born and raised in one specific belief system, would do what is necessary to explore other views and beliefs. If for instance your mother or father's occupation was that of a mill worker, a very respectable field of work, it does not imply that you must become a mill worker like them. In fact, it is very likely that your parents or any parent would want you to grow to greater heights through education and training. Why then do we limit ourselves and close the door on our mental growth by pigeonholing ourselves into one belief system? In doing so, we literally shut off the experience of what life shouts out to us daily. You change, life changes, we evolve! The unwavering commitment to a specific religious creed literally shuts down our natural curiosity to discover new ways to experience life. Often we rely on the subtleties of what we term faith. Faith being the knowledge that we do not and cannot know everything helps us to deal with conflicting facts or overloads of information. Where we encounter bad faith, is when we surrender our desire to explore and understand reality in spite of 'givens' or pre-supposed knowledge. In this respect, we quickly categorize things or events as something we should simply accept and never question.

What makes our religions or belief systems so credulous that it has limited our curiosity of the world around us? Siddhārtha Gautama commonly known as the Buddha, felt humanity's suffering occurred due to the false identity of the mind with the ego and self. In essence, the not knowing who and what we are has caused a split mind within us. The psychologist Carl Jung also felt this split mind or "ruptured self" was the cause of many of today's mental conditions. In a world where humanity often asks the question, why do we seem so intent in working against our fellow human beings? One can be quickly overwhelmed with conflicting answers before understanding the complexity of asking such a question in the first place. Are we asking this question from a basis of wisdom or fear? Fears such as; perhaps the world is an arbitrary, chaotic, senseless place, or maybe these questions are way beyond my understanding so it is best not to ask. Yet, when humanity does not honestly address these issues, we create this split mind within ourselves. Does this split in our mind create only larger issues for us? If we look at some statistics in the area of mental health, we find there is an estimated 26.2 percent of Americans ages 18 and older—about one in four adults—suffering from a diagnosable mental disorder in any given year. This figure translates to 57.7 million people! Further, approximately 2.5 million individuals suffer from schizophrenia, anxiety disorders, panic disorders, post-traumatic stress disorder and many other illnesses. Mental disorders are the leading cause of disability in the West, and many people suffer from more than one disorder at any given time. Approximately half of those with any one mental disorder exhibit two or more additional disorders. If these are the results of a split mind or psychic rupture, what have we done to ameliorate these problems?

The balm or bandage we have applied to heal this split has often come to us through our religions and spiritual leaders. The question we must now ask ourselves is whether this bandage has become tattered or is no longer useful. A larger understanding of *who* we are as human beings is required. To begin, our definition of god sorely needs revisiting. Metaphorically speaking, if an apartment building or public structure through abuse or neglect has fallen into disrepair it is often better to knock it down and build anew. It makes little sense as Jesus Christ of the Bible stated, to place new wine in old wineskins. Instead of using old definitions and descriptions, let us begin to create our own understanding of what this being is we have called god. Up to this point, our definition of god has been that of an all-powerful, all-knowing incorporeal *being* that has created our world and all its environs. Our dilemma in believing this is that why would an all-powerful *being* allow humanity's suffering or the existence of evil? Thomas Aquinas a 13th century philosopher and saint argued that our freedom of choice is a greater good than the lack thereof. Yet, the counter argument to this is that an all-powerful *being* could easily spare us from the process, allow us free will and eliminate all evil. Others would also argue that there is a Grand Plan or some larger blueprint from the beginning of time, and that this Grand Plan would guide humanity from its potential to its actual. Again, the counter argument to this is that any Grand Plan beforehand would inherently confine us to the freedom it offers. In essence, we would be limited to the plan.

There exists many compelling philosophical arguments for or against the existence of a divine *being*, and it would serve the curious reader to spend some time reading more on this subject. But as previously mentioned, many of these arguments and beliefs have run their course and will not serve us in coming to a new and better understanding of *who* and *what* we are. Taking a step back, one of the chapters of this book called *My God! You are God*, likely seemed provocative to you at first glance. The implication of equating human beings, society or even you to that of an all-powerful, all-knowing *being* is certainly intimidating! Yet here rests our error, based on humanity's splintering of consciousness, we have separated out our innate knowledge (god), then obfuscated its meaning. The question is not whether there is a god or not, the debate though interesting serves us no purpose. Rather, who is this strange species called humanity that has a need to believe in an all-powerful, all knowing *being*? If we can step away from the belief in an all powerful, all knowing *being* as a prerequisite to our existence, we may then begin to see the reason why we have created such.

Historically, humanity had to deal with the dangers and uncertainties of a large and often hostile world as well as, cope with many of life's mysteries. Associated shrines, rituals and sacred spots dating as far back as the Bronze Age, are equivalent to our current churches and places of worship. These historic places of worship served to comfort us in interpreting the more pervasive mysteries of birth, death and existence. Additionally, the belief in an external deity would help us reconcile the inexplicable natural disasters of life such as storms, floods, earthquakes and other environmental changes. From these beliefs, our metaphysical concept of god became a reality to us. By not perceiving the world and its environs as a part of what we are, a split between our intuitive mind and our logical mind occurred. This split further deepened as humanity began to appreciate its intellectual capacity and the higher aesthetics of life such as beauty, art and culture. One can only imagine an early human's reaction to watching a close friend or lover walking, talking and sharing food, then suddenly one day no longer moving, no longer alive. His or her recourse in mourning their fallen comrade, lover or mate was to believe that a transcendent experience had taken place. A transcendent belief in a larger experience or mythological significance created their physical world. Early humanity's knowledge of the natural world leads them down the external path or mythology of life. In essence, we have placed the external world full of its circumstances and various states of mind as an *a priori*, a priority above the intuitive world of perception. This world for humanity became the world of action and physical relationships. These physical relationships arduously analyzed, became the fundamental building blocks of our perceived reality. From the time of Rene Descartes, the French mathematician and philosopher known for his words "I Think, therefore I am," Western thought has found itself in the constant act of disassembling nature. This was a quest to find its constituent or fundamental parts. In modern times we see this split mind enacted in our daily approach to understanding life and each other.

In essence, the logical mind takes hold of the object or act, death in the case of our example above, while the intuitive mind desires to be one with it. If we move through time to modern indigenous tribes and peoples, we see the emergence of the farmer, humanity's early stage of managing their environment through agriculture. *Beings* such as The Fertility Mother, The Great Rainbow Snake and a myriad of other entities took on deified meanings in which humans identified themselves with animal, plant and natural phenomena. Tribal beliefs based on agriculture and farming became replete throughout Asia, Middle America, Mexico and southeast Europe. We see the Aborigine's Dreamtime, the American Indian's Wakan Tanka (Big Holy) and numerous primordial spirits and relations linked to a particular place or settlement. Here we see humanity connecting to its intuitive self through their immediate environment, and bridging the gulf between the reasoning mind and the intuitive mind. These peoples and cultures were closer to understanding the larger *self* by envisioning the individual as directly connected to the world around them.

In today's vast array of technologies and tools, we find the rift between our intuitive mind and logical mind growing. This form of external power, that which can be held in one's hands or kept in ones bank account, is no different than that of our early ancestor's bounty from a good hunt or day of gathering. It is from this survival perspective that we have offloaded our transcendent mind to a divinity that handles the burden of what we have not reconciled. In many eastern religious cultures, this split is consciousness identifying itself with a body. The Bhagavad-Gita, the comparable holy book of Hinduism, touches on this when Arjuna asks Krishna, why does man work against his own will through evil deeds? Krishna replies:

". . . Intellect, sense and mind
Are fuel to its fire:
Thus it deludes
The dweller in the body.
Bewildering his judgment."[2]

---

2. Swami Prabhavananda and Christopher Isherwood, *The Song of God Bhagavad-Gita*, (New York: New American Library, 1972), p. 17.

The overwhelming conclusion humanity has come to, is that the physical world perceived by the mind is the center of consciousness. The 19th century philosopher Immanuel Kant asked and answered this question in saying that all of our knowledge is rooted in the physical realms. According to Kant, these realms of space and time cannot exist if they do not first exist in the non-physical realms of the mind. When modern humanity elevated the physical realm to *a priori*, we set in motion a new way of perceiving the world by elevating causal law to the same level of intuitive thought. In essence, the split away from the intuitive mind not only separated us from our true self, it also confined us to these self-same rules. We have not only identified the self to that of our physical manifestation, we have systematically created a protagonist and a supporting cast of antagonists that also follow the same laws assigned to them by us.

This conceptual misunderstanding of reality is not attributable to the many great spiritual leaders society has come to acknowledge. Buddha consciousness speaks to the getting to know who you are as an awakened individual. Christ consciousness is that of unification of self, the father and son as one. In the Taoist view, we see life's interpretation as a mode of *being* versus an act. In a very interesting statement by Alan Watts' in his book titled *The Book*, we read: "We do not come into this world, we come out of it, as leaves from a tree."[3] The illusion we are under, that of an external deity, precipitates from the split within ourselves. Joseph Campbell, a well-known scholar on the mythological roots of human history stated: "Deities are symbolic personifications of the very energies that are of yourself."[4] How then do we experience this splitting of self in everyday life? One of the most common sentiments expressed by the individual is that of taking credit for the things done right, and placing blame on others or circumstances when things go wrong. The obvious contradiction here is that we see ourselves as a creative

---

3. Alan Watts, *The Book*, (New York: Vintage Books, 1989), p. 9.
4. Joseph Campbell, *Transformations of Myth Through Time*, (New York: Harper & Row, 1990), p. 106.

force in one instance, and then unwittingly denounce the same ability in the next moment.

This mode of thought perception ingrained in us from childhood, probably dates back to earlier times in history. It is obvious that our split consciousness has caused us to compartmentalize one side of our *being* as that of a logical creature and on the other, we create instinctual beliefs. In the world of psychology, thinkers such as Sigmund Freud saw religion as an illusion that served as a buttress against our more instinctual nature. In essence, he felt that our innate animal nature is a negative character trait as it relates to the more "Civilized" man. Carl Jung also saw religion as a replacement of humanity's primary archetypes. These archetypes represented the mythologized human psyche in organized and symbolic patterns. In order to keep track of our splintered selves, humanity has created a deity to help us make sense of the external world. A balanced or enhanced relationship between the logical and intuitive mind is required, for the intellect works with the intuitive mind in order to flourish. As the English Philosopher John Locke put it, reason is the judge of revelation. For what we see around us today is the intellect refusing to accept the possibility that there is more that composes the human animal than intellect alone. This mode of intellectual belief relentlessly reiterated and reinforced through the five-senses has for humanity become indisputable knowledge. From this world perspective of external reality only, the intellect must function without the compassion of the gentler aspects of the psyche. Instead of utilizing the enormous ability to think and work through the complex issues we face in today's world, we have often used this ability on one another in brutal and cruel ways. What then is required to unify the mind of humanity? Before we can mend or heal this split, we need to address our responsibility to our self and the wider world.

As creatures of reason and logic, it seems unreasonable to state that every thought, desire and event in the entire universe has some association with the individual. The reason this seems unfathomable is that you are attempting to understand this from an external or ego centered perspective. If we take a brief look at what is happening inside our own physical bodies, we see millions of biological activities occurring simultaneously and effortlessly. Within your nervous system alone, neurons are receiving and relaying thousands of tiny electrical signals to control and coordinate all essential functions of your body. Even if we do not take into account the work of the digestive system, the musculoskeletal system, the respiratory system and other networked systems, it is a wonder in and of itself that you are alive and reading these words. This physical manifestation called you, whether fathomable in its entirety or not, *is* who you are!

Your logical mind understands moment-to-moment events in your surroundings, while your intuitive mind insures you can function while doing so. It would seem foolish to a sixth grader or ten year old to say that our digestive system is a divine entity. Yet, we are doing exactly that by separating out the hard to explain mysteries and defining them as an unknown creator. In many philosophies of the East, it is believed that when the mind splits its logical side takes precedence. When the intuitive mind and logical mind are working together, the realization of your connection to everything including external events becomes internal. This is not a realization of supernatural power, it is a seeing of what has never been separate. In his book *The Tao of Physics,* Fritjof Capra explains this when he compares Eastern thought with Western thought and modern day Physics. What Mr. Capra discovered was that there exists a real web of inter-connectedness in all things. This he analogized with modern theories of quantum fields, Relativity and S-Matrix's to that of Eastern mysticism, meditative practices and non-dualistic thinking. What he saw was that everything in the universe connects to everything else in the universe. This connectivity to all things inside you and of you is the all-knowing intelligence we have mistakenly attributed to an external creator.

Based on the degree that you are consciously and emotionally in rapport with this inner intelligence, is to the same degree you are able to work with it. The biblical stories of walking on water or parting a sea would not be perceived as an external power, but rather a deep and clear understanding of the internal power that is within you. In his book *Ageless Body, Timeless Mind*, Deepak Chopra explains how our perceived Reality is that from which we draw our sense of power. In essence, if we base our reality on the external world of objects, then our base of power must primarily reside in the material world. It would then seem obvious that all our thoughts, opinions and abilities would be limited or confined to the material world. The numerous conflicts that consume our daily life are the residual effect of this split perspective. What are the conflicts we encounter in understanding true power? Let us list a few:

1. Attributing the cause or effect to that of an external power,
2. Perceiving the event from a split mind perspective and,
3. Fear of the loss of self or essence of our being.

Let us address each of these in detail. As previously discussed, we have induced ourselves into believing in the external physical world as *a priori*. This physical world by design must also include a deity as a primary cause. In this sense, we perceive power as a force not an essence. Humanity stands in awe at the great feats we have accomplished through natural or manufactured means and have called this power. True power though is not a force visited on another person, place or thing. What we have learned from history is that true power is a subtle presence, similar to a stream of water that takes countless millennia to carve a path through solid rock. It is in the unnoticeable events that allow a rose to bloom, and the almost unfathomable time and coordination of events required by humanity to reach this stage of self-awareness. True power cannot and does not need to force itself into *being* or existence. Through an awareness of our connectivity with everything, a subtle web of complimentary and synchronous agreements take place before true power occurs.

This is the case for every moment of your life whether it is walking up a flight of stairs, eating, breathing or simply reading these words. These daily occurrences and many other natural events of our lives, we do not consider miraculous or supernatural. If we extend this understanding to that of the external world as something intimately connected to us like a hand or arm, it would not seem strange to pick up a tree, stop a flowing river or move a mountain. The thought here is not whether this ability is available to you or not rather, what we must ask is that without the full knowledge of the many interrelationships involved in doing so, would it be similar to placing your hand in an open fire and expecting positive results. Dr. Wayne Dyer in his book *Manifest Your Destiny* explains our intrinsic connectivity to the environment around us when he writes:

> "Try thinking of the external world, your environment, as your extended body. That is, you are not separate from the external world you see. In this concept it is impossible to describe yourself without including your surroundings.
> In fact, it is not even possible to see or hear yourself as a separate entity apart from your environment."[5]

In Mr. Dyer's words, we *are* our environment and not a separate entity contending with separate distinct events. Understanding our true power in this context allows us to begin to understand the complex relationships and agreements that are a part of us. Power to move a mountain or part a sea for effect or fancy is excessive arrogance at its best. Doing this without understanding the myriad of life forms, their goals, needs and intentions, would only exhibit a powerful recklessness. This would appear no different to an onlooker watching you stand in triumph while purposefully doing harm to yourself. Our current perception of what power is if enacted in its full breadth, would unleash tremendous problems in the world. In this respect, we need to understand what we are creating from this split-mind perspective.

We live in the sensory world of touch, taste, sound, sight and

5. Wayne Dyer, *Manifest Your Destiny*, (New York: Harper Collins, 1997), p. 37.

smell. Our physical senses enable our cognitive abilities to discern a sequence of events and perceive a natural order of change. In this respect, we can say that our world is overflowing with perceivers in the continuous act of perceiving someone or something. In an effort to analyze this perceptual phenomenon, we can attempt to categorize our modes of perceptions in two distinct ways. The first in which our perceptions occur on an automatic basis from learned behaviors e.g., walking, talking and those of cognitive perceptions found in problem solving and logic. A leisure stroll down an average city block requires an automatic evaluation and re-evaluation of a multitude of sights, sounds and spatial events. These perceptions occur without the reflective state or attitude commonly found in cognitive thought processes. In this sense, the world we perceive on an average city block is a world of learned likelihoods and expectancies. If we evaluate the human body in this manner, we can also say we provide ourselves with constant feedback on our individual appearance and state of mind without conscious effort. If we equate the body to that of the ego, we can say that the ego-model of ourselves, in a less physical sense, continuously receives updates with new sensory information.

When this new information is perceived, additional analysis into the nature of this space-time event is required. In this respect, our cognitive abilities in the area of problem solving, memory and intuition are used. An object under perception whether living, non-living or an abstract thought during cognitive analysis, lends its static existence to that of the perceiver. In essence, the object exists based on your subconscious belief in its existence and conscious belief in its function. If for instance I attribute all the qualities of this book to that of a clock, its existence and function becomes and is exactly that for me. If we take this analogy a little further, the turning of one of its pages could easily represent parcels of time, or an altogether new concept of time. One might experience time based on the emotional response felt after reading each page. Although this example would mentally place us in radically different universes, modern science has shown that this is not far from the case.

Science has provided us with insight into the subatomic world of atoms, electrons, protons and a host of other smaller particles. In essence, our concrete world of subatomic particles moving at near light-speeds comprises all physical matter. These scientific representations allude to a world in constant flux whose dynamics describe a primordial *soup* of energies, and much less the apparent physical reality we perceive. In reality, our material world eludes its perceiver. Also within our material world, we encounter the non-linear perceiver where a leap in logic such as the gravitational bending of light perceived by Einstein, provided us with the laws of relativity. Now we see modern science struggling to understand the world of quantum physics. Quantum physicists tell us that physical matter can exhibit the qualities of being in two places at the same time. They describe the actual event that is happening is directly related to the observer. This tells us that what you perceive is occurring, occurs at the point of perception! These discoveries do not obey our earlier premise of a concrete world rather they allude to the conclusion that we perceive at a non-concrete speed a non-concrete world. The question must then be asked, does our perception define our reality and if so to what degree? Without entertaining any questions concerning the definition of the word *reality,* which we will cover in later chapters, let us take a hard look at the conclusions we have reached so far.

Our logical mind's belief in the five-sensory world as an *a priori*, expressed in sayings like "survival of the fittest", has led us to equate physical objects as centers of power. In understanding the physical world, we begin to see that we do not live in a physical realm but simply perceive it as such. In the recent popular movie, *The Matrix* starring Keanu Reeves, the main character demonstrated this when he was awakened from a fictitious world perception and had to confront a new paradigm of reality. Similarly, another character in the movie felt that the current reality was too overwhelming, and opted to return to the prior reality and its society of rules and power struggles. In both situations, their understanding of true power was an illusion based on their current understanding and beliefs. Humanity's current illusion of power, wealth, possessions and instant gratifications, are simply the ground rules created by us. Real power is not how we exert or force our wishes on another. In doing so, the personality is looking to justify its physical existence. The illusion of success in doing so temporarily disguises itself in the need for further physical gratification. This endless need for gratification of the self occurs because its physical requirements remain inexhaustible. Based on our high investment in this illusion of split-minded reasoning, we ferociously cling to this perception at all costs. In his book *Essence of the Heart Sutra*, the Dalai Lama explains this when he writes:

> "On the whole, we naturally tend to trust our everyday perceptions we assume their validity without it ever occurring to us to question them. We naively believe that the way we perceive things is identical with the way things are. And so, because events and things, including the self, appear to have objective reality, we conclude, tacitly and often without any reflection at all, that they do in fact have an objective reality. Only through the process of careful analysis can we see that this is not so, that our perceptions do not accurately reflect objective reality."[6]

Very much like the main character in the movie *The Matrix*, in the back of our mind we are haunted with the knowledge there exists an objective reality we are not experiencing. Our term and definition to explain or define this feeling we have called god. Based on the conclusion that god is beyond our intellectual comprehension, it then logically makes sense for us to believe in an unknown.

Up to this point, we have touched on the subject of power understood as an external force and our perception of it from a focused

---

6. Dalai Lama, *Essence of the Heart Sutra*, (Boston: Wisdom Publications, 2002), p. 101.

split mind perspective. Before we look at the more complex area of *what* and *who* we are, let us take a brief look at the *mind* of humanity. As a species on planet earth, our unique ability to think, reflect and assimilate information, is psychologically attributed to what we call our conscious and subconscious minds. We define the conscious mind as the functioning individual and the subconscious mind as the intuitive state of mind found in dreams, desires and impulses. Additionally, memory serves us in relating disparate events and past images to our present self. In essence, we attribute our identity to a succession of interrupted events, scattered imaginations and reactive behaviors. Our current understanding is that these states of mind come from both the conscious and subconscious processes. It is also evident that anything consciously reflected on for any length of time becomes part of the subconscious mind. Psychiatrists have attributed many of our mental aberrations or *complexes* to this form of habitual patterning. The conscious mind clearly exhibits its power in its ability to discern and then categorize its perceptions.

These discernments or thoughts, then become a part of the 'who we are' from a conscious and subconscious basis. In his book *Science of the Mind*, Ernest Holmes elaborates on the power of conscious thought as that of an inner movement based on our perceptions and our reactions to them. He further describes this ability as the same force that creates everything including the smallest microbe to the planets and the stars. The only limitation in fully working with or utilizing this power rests within our understanding of it. If we agree with Mr. Holmes, our prior understanding of an 'objective reality' as also described by the Dalai Lama is larger than imagined. Can we now state that our thoughts not only create our beliefs and perceptions but also our physical reality? We see this in the many individuals around us who through determination, motivation and intention have impressed their subconscious minds to create great works in the arts and sciences. Their ability to develop a clear understanding of the operations and the powers of the intuitive mind, allowed them to create the external world according to their inner worlds. Every intention is energy in motion and is the primary cause of each moment we live on every level of our reality.

Creative thought as conduit to conscious existence and experience, is the foundation of this reality we call life. Your reality is the result of your own unconscious beliefs and conscious intentions. Although we have been distinguishing the conscious mind from the subconscious, there is really only one mind and the spectrum through which it is used. Instead of working towards integrating our conscious processes with our larger selves, we have placed both at a distance to one another. This likely occurred during early childhood where issues of conformity and security took precedence over natural growth and change. A negative reaction to the statement that you *have* created everything in your world: body, mind, personality, dreams, shortcomings etc, . . . exemplifies the fact that you see your conscious mind as a sole power broker. Ironically, whether you believe you have self-created this individual called you or not, you are right in both cases. You, the conscious thinker or ego has not, but the larger 'you', the intuitive mind, has. The issue we come up against is how then does the mind find any consensus of reality? In other words, how can all of us create our reality separately and individually at the same time? Let us examine what we now term our 'consensus reality' and how we relate to it.

As humans, we require that a book, clock or door exist *for us* in order to perceive it. Further, a plausible assumption of its function *to us* must exist relative to the world we inhabit. Whether its existence is a tangible reality or not is not important. A simple but effective way for insuring that our mode of perception is not *off-kilter* is to utilize previous experience, memory and logic as a reference. We also on occasion obtain a mutual consensus from another that what we perceive is the same event or object for them. In essence, a *clock, you* and *I* are relative existents dependent on each other, and our agreement to it being a *clock* is necessary. The object under perception must lend its static existence to that of the perceiver, in that its existence is a function of belief. We can further say that this is the case when both objects are in a position to perceive each other. If we rigorously adhere to this line of reasoning, we fall into a black hole of perceptions. What we would experience is a world populated in exclusion by perceivers without any consensus of a mutual reality. Since this is not the case, we must explore the concept of common references as it relates to perception.

In 1954 Doctor John C. Lilly, a pioneer in Brain and Behavior based studies, began experimenting with the concept of restricting the amount of external sensory stimuli to the brain. Using isolation or flotation tanks, individuals experienced a state with normal environmental stimuli removed. These tests have shown that an individual's mind undergoes a disassociation of what we have termed the concrete world, and functions at a more optimal capacity. Similarly, during later night periods of REM sleep, Rapid Eye Movement, dream synthesis and plot is less associated with normal waking reality. These tests and findings point to the fact that a stable reference is necessary to insure we perceive a common worldview. In essence, we need to be in a position to perceive an earth in order to perceive a sky. Further, what is required is a multitude of stable references in order to relate to each other and the world around us.

The relationship of perceiver-to-perceived is further complicated when an object viewed at various timeframes or mental states is perceived as an entirely different object. Perception in this sense has undergone a radical change in that the book has become the clock or vice versa. Finally, the object under perception may also undergo change where the perceiver may or may not attribute new qualities to the object. Following this line of logic of perceiver-to-perceived, we can make a statement to the effect that the observer and observed are dependent on one another and not separate events. This speaks to our earlier statement that our unity is a reality of mutually agreed on relationships. We also see this concept fully expressed in the scientific world. The scientific concept called *complementarity* implies the impossibility of a sharp separation between the behavior of a system and its interaction with the observer, usually identified as the wave-particle duality. This opens the door too mutual dependencies where science has stepped beyond its world of empirical knowledge and pragmatism. What we begin to hear from our scientists is that of probabilities and statistical possibilities. Physical matter as we have understood from a Newtonian perspective is an interaction of measurements, and no longer a separate phenomenon.

This physical world as currently discussed by scientists is that of *frozen energy,* an e*nergy* that becomes another form when subjected to the right impetus or quantum *push.* An analogy would be that of water becoming steam when heated or ice when cooled. What then would produce a sufficient quantum *push* to move a mountain or part a sea? It is the same force maintaining the millions on millions of functions happening within your body right now. We have mistakenly attributed the lion share of *what* and *who* we are to that of the conscious mind or ego. The unified mind or total individual extends beyond the understanding of ego awareness. In the words of Carl Jung:

> "The psyche is the world's pivot: not only is it the one great
> condition for the existence of a world at all, it is also an
> intervention in the existing natural order, and no one can
> say with certainty where this intervention will finally end."[7]

With an understanding of what this mental split is, and how perception creates these external events, it is time we look at what we have created. There is a well-known historical event concerning Christopher Columbus's journey to the New World. As his ships approached the New World and became visible on the horizon from the shore a strange event occurred. The native's on shore, completely unfamiliar with large sea going vessels, simply could not see his ships. They noticed only the ripple and turbulence of water caused by something at a distance in the water. After some time, a shaman

---

7. Carl G. Jung, *The Undiscovered Self,* (New Jersey: Princeton University Press, 1990), p. 127.

from another local village finally saw the ships for what they were, and expressed this to the rest of his tribe. This story speaks to the probability and likelihood that our deeply held beliefs in a linear world of cause and effect may be turbulence on the water, and not the real or true nature of things. We have discussed how consensual reality takes place in a mode of collective agreements. It is through these consensual agreements that society can limit its beliefs and logical paradigms to an acceptable reality.

Understanding that our rules and logical paradigms provide us with the guideposts for helping us understand ourselves, they have also become the barriers to seeing *what* and *who* we truly are. What then are the reasons we limit our perceptions in this manner? Society and the individual create these barriers in order to protect its fragile sense of self. We have invested heavily in believing that we as individuals are our private lives of beliefs, memories, habits and possessions. The fallout from this mode of belief is that we have created an emptiness or hollowness in our individual and collective psyches. Eventually, this state of emptiness and self-imposed assumptions becomes the fear of the unknown. Jean-Paul Sartre a well-known philosopher had made the statement, "Man is the *Being* through which Nothingness enters the world". Sartre believed that man invents a god in order to account for meaning in the world. Humanity's emptiness or cosmic meaningless, drives us to invent a concept that can explain these mysteries including the origin of the world. Rene Descartes also spoke to this quality of human reality as that which burdens out Nothingness and called it freedom. The freedom to be the essence of our own existence as conduit and creator dictates both enormous possibility and responsibility. As an analogy, it would be similar to suddenly waking up and finding yourself in command of a massive airliner without the knowledge on how to pilot it. Our individual egos thrust into an unfamiliar circumstance, one in which established mental constructs are abstracted, would be overwhelmed with the situation and quickly withdraw or dissolve.

The ego's constant need to maintain control serves as both the measure of its inability to cope with reality and its frailty. The tendency of the ego is therefore to cling to the belief of an enduring reality for its safety. Our misunderstanding of self lies in the belief that we are this enduring person, state, attitude and personal history of X number of years, months and days. In David Hawkins book *I - Reality and Subjectivity*, he expresses this when he states:

> "The 'me' that is so jealously guarded and cherished is an elaborate series of layers of programs of which the last underlying program to be undone is that the other layers of programs are real and 'myself'. . . The fear of nonexistence then arises, followed by the fear of death itself, for it is only the illusory self that is subject to actual death."[8]

Throughout history, philosophers, sages and thinkers have expressed to us that the mistake we make as individuals is in associating our true nature to that of the personal self. The tenacious battle over our embedded sense of self according to Buddhist writings is the source of our suffering. Similarly, the words of Christ speak to the humility of the personal self, relinquishment of greed and avarice with a goal towards a unified psyche. These thinkers understood that our personal ego obscured our true nature and reality. Our true self harbors no obsessions, disorganizations, conflicts or emotional instabilities.

How then do we begin to realize our true self? What guideposts if any can we look to for making a radical change from seeing the ego as self? What can or should we believe in and why? In the next chapter of this book we will discuss several different viewpoints that may run hard against the grain of accepted beliefs and social mores. These new guideposts will aid us in laying the groundwork towards a better understanding of *what* and *who* we are.

---

8. David R. Hawkins, *I Reality and Subjectivity*, (Arizona: Veritas Publishing, 2003), p. 52.

2
New Rules

"Curious people are interesting people, I wonder why that is?"
—Bill Maher

In a popular weekly TV show called *Real Time with Bill Maher*, the host Bill Maher finishes the show with a short diatribe he entitles "New Rules". During his tongue-in-cheek commentary on the state of affairs in the world, more often than not his words cut closer to the truth than one would ever care to admit. In a similar fashion, this chapter will take a no holds barred approach in laying out some new understandings that may not sit well with current beliefs. In our previous chapter, we discussed the reasons behind our psychic split from the natural world from both a historical and physical perspective. We saw that our alignment with the ego-personality, as the primary power broker of our world, created tremendous discord for humanity. In this respect, what we discovered was that we have off-loaded our true self, our intuitive nature, for causal laws and beliefs. We have created complex systems and processes for maintaining and controlling our world of contradictions, falsehoods and misconceptions. In an attempt to clarify these "New Rules," we must be careful to avoid statements that refer to a *given,* or a simple because we have always believed it to be so. Better said in the words of the philosopher Denis Diderot:

"If nature offers us a difficult knot to unravel, do not let us introduce in order to unravel it the hand of a *being* who then becomes an even more difficult knot to untie than the first one."[1]

Using the above sentiment as a guidepost, let us start this section with our first "New Rule".

A. There is only one of us

Our basic assumption about ourselves has been that we are individuals made up of our individual memories, thoughts, personal history, likes, dislikes, beliefs, race, creed, sex, body and so on. This sense of self we call by proper name; Mike, Mary, Yusuf, Sam, Fatima, Chin is exactly that, a 'sense' of self. We hold precious this very private self and assume it is who we are as individuals. If we look at the meaning of the word personality, we see it comes from the Latin root *persona*, which means the mask worn over the actor or being. This mask bears the features, traits, characteristics and roles we live by including hero, thief, saint and sinner. Heinrich Zimmer, a student of Indian literature, comments on the meaning of this word as follows:

> "The word connotes that the personality is but the mask
> of one's part in the comedy or tragedy of life and not to
> be confused with the actor. It is not a manifestation of his
> true nature, but a veil."[2]

In this sense, the individual self or person is a reusable mask or prop worn for a time then discarded. In Jungian psychology, this collection of masks or props might be termed humanity's collective unconsciousness. This collective unconsciousness, as further

---

1. Denis Diderot, *Promenade of a Skeptic – The Walk of the Skeptic,* (Completed but not published, 1747), p. 28.
2. Heinrich Zimmer, *Philosophies of India,* (New York: Meridian, 1956), p. 236.

defined by Jung, is an expendable form within the mind of humanity that remains always present and available for reuse. We can extrapolate from this description that a person or personality, represents the non-physical component of the physical representation of the *self*. The *self* as defined here is that of a symbolic or metaphorical counterpart of the mind, and its structure is that of an energetic pattern or framework of symbols within the collective consciousness. This collective repository of forms, motifs, roles and props, when pulled out of storage and worn by the individual, is what we now define as the ego. The problem we have with understanding this reality is the realization that everything we currently hold as real and personal about ourselves is impermanent. This simple yet enigmatic truth evidenced in countless cultures, myths and writings throughout the ages, has caused humanity great confusion on the meaning of the *self*. In an almost playful way, the Greeks, Egyptians, Romans and many other cultures, represented this knowledge by seeing the individual as an ensemble of gods, goddesses or animal presences.

Behind this façade of masks, many cultures felt there existed one thinking *I*, that was feeling and remembering everything experienced by the individual. In the writings of theologian Paul Tillich, he calls this the "Ultimate Ground of Being". In essence, Mr. Tillich felt there is no other person, place or thing perceiving reality. What modern humanity has done was to categorize our individual traits then bundle them up in a tidy package of emotional attitudes and beliefs. Yet, this is not 'who you are', your true self as expressed by countless traditions is this *I* we have called god. If we substitute the word *I* as follows; in Buddhism we would hear; you are the 'I' (Buddha). In the Yogic tradition, we would read 'I' (God) is within you and is you, and in the Islamic faith we would read that knowing your true self is 'I' (God). What these many faiths and philosophers realized was that in addition to our natural physical existence, our true self was a single *being*. As further expressed in the words of the Austrian Physicist Erwin Schrodinger:

On Being the Being

> "... the self-consciousness[es] of the individual members are numerically identical both with [one an] other and with that Self which they may be said to form at a higher level."[3]

Our confusion occurs in seeing and believing in a separate self, overlord of selves or individual self. The belief of a super *I* gave rise to humanities belief in a multitude of little *"I's"* and individuals. Living with this illusion, we fancy a supreme or universal ego as an absolute reality. Projecting our belief to an ultimate personal entity or ego is as fundamentally an illusion as identifying with an individual ego or personality.

What we have called or term this super single self, Spirit, God, Krishna, Buddha, The Higher Self, etc., ... is unimportant. The understanding that our true self is a singular *I* of *being,* and not a separate entity is a more accurate understanding. In many Asian philosophies, we find this unity of *being* in their views on nature. In essence, they subscribe to the belief that there exists an extensive cooperation of all *beings* and things misinterpreted as a separate hierarchy of selves. In many other belief systems, everything in the universe exists as intimately connected events such that no single separate part exists. It is felt that when consciousness fully encounters this from an experiential basis, an interpenetration of *being* occurs beyond the confines of language. The Buddhist perspective on this takes us a step further in seeing this interpenetration as the all-within-all. From a Buddhist worldview, this is the entire universe existing within a grain of sand. Beyond the current metaphysical views of this interconnectivity, modern physicists are now seeing that their search for the basic building blocks of nature has been misguided. What scientists are discovering is that all forms of matter are fluid and ever changing. In lab experiments, particle collisions have shown that the results leftover from a collision amounted

---

3. Erwin Schrodinger, *My View of the World,* (Connecticut: Ox Bow Press, 1983), pp. 31-34.

to more than the original constituent particles could account for. What they have also discovered was that particle resultants were dependent on *their* origin constituents. As an example of this, we see the resultant particles (K+) and ($\prod$-) from a collision produces a ($\sum$-) and a (K+) particle with a Neutron participating in the center as shown below (Diagram A):

Particle Collision(s)

Diagram A

Diagram B

List Of Particles In above examples

P = Proton $\sum$- = Sigma Λ = Lambda Baryon
$\prod$- = Pion K+ = Kaon

In Diagram B, we see the same interaction but the Proton (P) is part of a prior set of interactions (K+) and (Λ). What we are seeing here is the inklings of a much larger network of interactions that can precede any event. What is unique about Diagram B is that the Neutron in the center is participating in both reactions in an integrated fashion. This points to the fact that all matter as we fundamentally understand it, is not a given quantity but an interconnected web of mutual relationships.

The problem we encounter with realizing this center-less *I* of *being,* is in our ingrained belief in a dualistic universe. A belief system based on opposites such as up vs. down, cold vs. hot, good vs. bad and so on. What we are finding is that there are no opposite relations rather, only gradations that exist on a human made scale of measurements. Based on this causal belief system, the concept of simultaneity, two things existing or occurring in the same place at the same time, we perceive as a paradox. If we use the commonly accepted scientific understanding of Light Waves, we see Light exists as both wave and particle. Metaphorically speaking, can we say that our true self as a single "*I*" is simultaneously experienced as individual personalities and is still singular? According to Indian Vedanta texts, the identity of the individual is the nature of pure consciousness, a state of awareness beyond all opposites or dualities. Our fear of forfeiting our sense of uniqueness in lieu of a single "*I*" is the ego's confusion that it exists as a separate entity. In experiencing ourselves as a separate ego and personality, we can clearly express to another individual when we feel happy, sad or angry. Nevertheless, it is a little odd that we cannot recognize that these emotions occur for others as the same emotion! You can only emotionally experience something as it relates to you as one *I* can experience them. In his book *Dialogue with Death*, Eknath Easwaran expresses this best when he writes:

> "The Self in each of us is one and the same. For this Self,
> different names are given in different traditions . . . In
> this sense, life is a kind of cosmic condominium with
> billions of apartments, each with a different name on the
> door yet each with the same occupant."[4]

By seeing the self as a unified *being,* it becomes possible to rise above the awareness of the individual who sees many trees but not the forest. In summary, and as humorously expressed by the comedian Lily Tomlin, we can begin to agree with her when she stated, "We are all in this, by ourselves."

B. We are not alive

The illusion of the persona or personal ego requires a contextual reality and framework to support it. This contextual reality or ego

---

4.   Eknath Easwaran, *Dialogue With Death*, (California: Nilgiri Press, 1981), pp. 169-170.

state of perceiving is what we have called being alive, but in reality we are not alive, we are life. Our split mind perspective has harbored this illusion of being alive by believing in a shadow existence. Plato, the well-known Greek Philosopher, summarized this in a short story where he describes humans sitting in a cave looking at shadows cast on the wall. Occasionally someone stands up and realizes that these are merely shadows, gets up and walks out of the cave into the daylight. This realization occurs for many individuals at the point of physical mortality when the illusion of ego-body-world begins to fade. Elisabeth Kubler-Ross a pioneer in the field of death, dying and the afterlife, saw this illusion unfold in many cases of terminally ill patients she worked with. In her book *On Life after Death,* she explains that physical death is similar to the shedding of a butterfly's cocoon. Rather than being perceived as an end to existence, she describes this process as that of putting away an old coat that has been worn-out, or is no longer needed when the season has changed. She further noted that a deep expansion of the individual occurs in the area of equanimity or resolution. This was not described as a point of surrender rather, a transition to another state of *being*.

Carl Jung in his extensive experience working with patients, also observed several individual's experiences up to the immediate presence of death. His conclusions were that dying had its onset long before the actual event, and that the individual personality underwent a process of transformation. What he saw was a resolution and loosening of the psyche or psychological structures of the ego-body-world relationship occur. One of his noted cases involved a very intelligent woman whose relationship with her family was very strained. During the process of her analysis and leading up to her final days, all her previous convictions and denials related to her family began to resolve themselves through periods of deep reflection. What startled Jung most about her case was that there was little if any concern by the unconscious mind over the personal death of the individual. It appeared to him that the unconscious mind of the individual simply did not care. In Jung's words:

> "It would seem as though death were something
> relatively unimportant, or perhaps our psyche does not
> bother about what happens to the individual. But it seems
> that the unconscious is all the more interested in how
> one dies that is whether the attitude of consciousness is
> adjusted to dying or not."[5]

Can we speculate that our personal egos adjusted during the process of death, evolves from a self-centered perspective? We know that from a physical basis every living plant, animal and microbe dramatically changes at the time of death. Other similar transformations such as a caterpillar into a graceful butterfly or a tadpole becoming a mature amphibian, occurs in a rapid timeframe. Additionally, many scientist and geneticist speculate that the birds of today were genetically at one time prehistoric dinosaurs! Based on these constant and dramatic changes, the individual organism adapts itself to a new or previously unknown environment. These conclusions would point back to Carl Jung and Elisabeth Kubler-Ross's observations that an adapted state of consciousness occurs at death.

From a medical perspective, doctors and health professionals more than any other group in society, are privy to the final days on earth of the terminally ill. In the book, *Psychiatric Aspects of Terminal Illness*, a number of medical professionals discuss the medical care of dying patients as well as, the patient's attitude and behavior during this stage of life. One problem noted by the many physicians in this book is the overly clinical approach used in dealing with patients during this final stage of their life. Doctor Allen Fertziger comments on this when he writes:

---

5. Carl G. Jung, *The Structure and Dynamics of the Psyche,* (New Jersey: Princeton University Press – The Bollingen Series, 1959), p. 411.

David Sutherland

"Foremost among the human spiritual qualities that have been eradicated from the modern materialist map is the spiritual substrate of subjective experience known as the human mind."[6]

He further suggests that we have:

". . . reached a point in our own professional development where we should   sidestep this ideological tyranny and establish our own maps that will more adequately describe the professional terrain we travel each day with our clients and colleagues."[7]

In addition to Doctor Fertziger, many medical professionals including neurosurgeon Wilder Penfield, Nobel Prize recipient Charles Sherrington, John Eccles and others adopted a view that there is a reality beyond physical existence. This separate existence, although not elaborated on in many scientific journals, has been widely accepted by cultures throughout time. Ancient Egyptian Priests, Tibetan Lamas, poets, philosophers, theologians and others have spoken of life after the body's existence ends. It is fascinating to note that science, modern humanity's materialistic guidepost, has all but approached this subject as taboo. What has 'gone missing' in modern medicine is the complimentary role of the physician as healer of body *and* mind. What we are beginning to see is a new form of compassionate healing taking place geared towards incorporating a number of integrative or holistic techniques.

The Asian healing art of Acupuncture based on the energy model of the entire human body, has become more widely accepted in the West. We also see a plethora of herbal products used to naturally cure or ameliorate diseases such as Alzheimer's, Osteoporosis, Diabetes and others. These and many other adaptive techniques assist

---

6. Allen Fertiziger, *Psychiatric Aspects of Terminal Illness,* (Philadelphia, The Charles Press, 1988) p. 161.
7. Ibid., p. 164.

in eliminating the patients' pain, suffering and disease on many different levels. Healing the energetic, physical, cellular, emotional and mental component of the individual is required in order to regain his or her state of health and well-being. As we begin to understand what the many doctors, caregivers and therapists of times past and present have learned, we realize that our personal *self* is not the individual fish in a body of water called life but life itself!

C. Nothing has ever occurred

The connotation of the meaning of the word 'nothing,' as it relates to our existence is often perceived in a negative connotation and avoided. We see the individual as a summation of events, memories and experiences, yet paradoxically we do not see these memories and experiences as the sole definition of *self* we have come to use. If we strip away all current, past and future reference to the individual self, the individual *I* simply cannot exist. The difficulty one has with the thought that *nothing* has occurred is due to our intransigent belief that we are things existing in a world of things. Within our focused existence or temporal reality, we have come to believe that events enter into *being* and eventually subside into *non-being*. The question of why does anything exist at all is seldom asked. If we take a strictly physical view of the universe, current theory tells us that down to the smallest fraction of a second, reality appeared as infinitesimally compact quantities of enormous energy. Eventually, these very compact quantities of energy lead to a great explosion we have called the Big Bang. Moving forward through history, this helps us explain the shaping of the past, present and future, but does not answer our original question of what caused even these infinitesimal compact energies to occur? Gottfried Leibniz, a scholar and philosopher of the 16th Century, offered us an answer to this question by describing a principle he termed 'Sufficient Reason.'. What he said was that nothing exists without sufficient reason or cause for its existence. What then created this sufficient reason, or caused this non-contingent *being*? This is exactly where Leibniz takes us in his theory, that of a necessary *Being* which remains outside of all contingencies.

As discussed in our guidelines and at the beginning of this chapter, Leibniz's premise limits us to the assumption of phenomena and so we must refute it. A non-contingent *being,* perceived by a contingent *being* is a trapdoor towards avoiding the question altogether. Immanuel Kant also refuted Leibniz's premise in his *Critique of Pure Reason.* He stated that to go beyond our sphere of experience in defining a non-contingent *being,* our concepts naturally fail to clearly prove or disprove it. Leibniz's premise does not negate the possibility of a non-contingent *being,* but does leave us with an abstraction at its very best. Even though it appears we live in a causal world, we need not surrender this paradox of existence based solely on sensory experience. Simply asking the question of why does anything exist at all? Can be answered with a simple 'one can never know', yet we can also try to approach the question from a different perspective.

Consciousness for all of us exists as a 'Consciousness of Content,' in essence the individual mind requires an object to perceive itself or another. Without the criteria of conscious content, there is no ability for reflective behaviors or self-consciousness. The mind of humanity must conceive of something in its inner dialogues in order to remain conscious. Better expressed by the philosopher Jean-Paul Sartre:

> "For consciousness there is no *being* except for
> this precise obligation to be a revealing intuition of
> something."[8]

In the absence of something, consciousness as experienced during non-REM sleep has no awareness of self or even a sense that

---

8. Jean-Paul Sartre, *Being and Nothingness,* (New York: Philosophical Library, 1956), p. 786.

there was a conscious self. Consciousness is enigmatic in that it exists only in lieu of objects or existents. Our conceptual nothing-ness knocks on the door of unconsciousness, pre-consciousness or non-existence.

When we speak of non-existence or nothingness, we open the door to all possibilities as well as, inclusively none. Correspond-ingly, the individual *I* of the question becomes the summation of all past, current and ongoing experiences. Where we encounter the conflicted individual on this point is in the connotation of nothing-ness being the fear of non-existence. From this understanding, and without placing moral value on the concept of non-existence, can we state that logically nothing has or ever will occur? This ques-tion challenges our common worldview with its myriad of physi-cal sights, sounds and sensations. If we state consciousness without content is this void, and the basis for all possibility is what human-ity continues to experience, how then do we explain our physical experience or this content of *being*?

When we begin to understand that this *being* of context is who we are and not its content, then as put in the words of Jean-Paul Sartre that; "Nothingness haunts being,"[9] becomes an accurate statement. From here, we can further say humans exist as this *being* of concep-tual nothingness. Again, understanding that our persona is a shadow of what we come to term our individual reality, the realization of what we call the physical world based on an illusion must also be an illusion. As eloquently expressed by Hsuan-Tsang in his Treatise called *The Establishment of the Doctrine of Consciousness-only*, we read:

> "Both the world and the sacred doctrines declare that the self and dharmas are merely constructions based on false ideas and have no reality of their own."[10]

---

9. Ibid., p. 12.
10. Hsuan-Tsang, *A Source Book in Chinese Philosophy*, (New Jersey: Princeton University Press, 1963), p. 374.

He then asks and answers our question in stating:

> "How do we know that there is really no sphere of
> objects but only inner consciousness which produces
> what seem to be the external spheres of objects? Because
> neither the real self nor the real dharma is possible." [11]

Dharma, as referenced in the above quote signifies the underlying order in nature. In essence, we have based our physical reality on the illusion that the ego model of self is real. If we metaphorically approach the above statement, we could say it is as if someone asked you what the man on the moon had for breakfast. The obvious answer is that the question is without merit based on its original premise being a falsehood.

Our investment in believing that an individual self exists has placed content above context. Context represents the framework beneath supporting elements against the universal backdrop. The ego can be described as the individual's content, and the unspecified or non-focused consciousness its context. Content in our physical surroundings are dependent on a non-physical medium such as the actual space between objects. This non-physical medium or void called space is the metaphysical nothingness of which we now define. In the flux of this medium, we can say that physical objects perceived by an individual might appear to originate through this void as a natural incongruity. In-depth analysis of this nothingness or void provides us with the insight that physical objects do not originate from it, but are a part of it. The philosopher Georg Hegel saw this non-*being* vs. *being* as two necessary components without making the *being* pass into nothingness. Martin Heidegger another philosopher on this matter commented that these were repulsive forces, whereas reality is somehow the tension resulting from their opposition. Finally, Jean Paul Sartre viewed the existence of non-*being* through its *being*. The common ground in their writings is in

11. Ibid., p. 375.

On Being the Being

the necessary relationship between *being* and non-*being* whether viewed concretely or contextually. In the next chapter we will take an in depth look at context and reality in which most if not all of our assumptions will be put to the test.

D. The next step

To understand what the next step in our process of evolution involves, we need to understand the process of what is taking place in this moment called *now*. We intuitively understand that in a short lapse of time our physical body will start to falter. Death can occur through natural means such as accidents or illnesses. Regardless of the cause, what we so intrinsically believed to be 'who we are', our bodies, minds and sense of self, will stop functioning. In the case of long-term illness or similar natural causes, each of us will enter into various stages of dying as detailed by the noted M.D. Elisabeth Kubler-Ross. In her working with the terminally ill of all ages, sexes and cultures, Kubler-Ross discovered and documented the five-stages of death we commonly refer to today. Elisabeth Kubler-Ross provided us a guide to the stages of dying or grieving which involved denial, anger, bargaining, depression and finally acceptance.

Her pioneering work in this field has helped countless individuals and families understand and work through this difficult process. As described in the final stage of death called acceptance, the dying individual begins to spend more time sleeping, as if in preparation for an extended transition. This has been noted and expressed as the final rest before a long journey. Additionally, the individual starts to feign the company of family, and often wishes to spend more time alone and undisturbed from the events of the outside world. In Kubler-Ross's experience, repetitive emotional and psychological patterns emerged during this stage. When physical illness is occurring, we see the mind of the individual open up to different states of consciousness. As also expressed by Kathleen Singh in her book *The Grace in Dying*, our identity begins a transformation or shift

43

from external references. A re-identification of the individual self with its noted habits, peculiarities and ways of thinking takes place. In Mrs. Singh's words:

> "Consciousness and identity have moved into dimensions that eclipse the tendency to place the locus of self in the physical / emotional / mental organism alone."[12]

What Mrs. Singh saw was that an expansion or dissolution of the ego-mind boundaries of self begins to occur. A non-archetypal level of *being* took precedence over the self as the individual consciousness withdrew from the physical world. This occurrence is evident in our earthly preparations of body and mind as we progress through various stages of life. As an example, as we grow from infancy to adolescence then adulthood and old age, perceptual awareness also changes or expands throughout these transitions. In order to begin the transition to the next stage of consciousness, possibly non-local awareness, the framework of a wider consciousness is required. As eloquently expressed by Mrs. Singh:

> "It is the first, still distorted, witnessing of Reality, involving suspension of all dualisms except some forms of the first Dualism, that of self versus not-self."[13]

As a possible cushion to brace the individual during this traumatic transition, we can speculate that a modified template of the ego-mind model is necessary. Humanity's premise of what we now define as reality becomes the perspective of an expanded consciousness. As an analogy, it would be difficult to describe the psychosexual passions of an adult to a pre-adolescent child without the pre-requisite of puberty. Words would only fall short in conveying

---

12. Kathleen Dowling Singh, *The Grace in Dying,* (San Francisco: Harper Collins, 2000), p. 78.
13. Ibid., p. 78.

what an adult's goals, passions and desires represent compared to the mindset of a child or infant.

At this stage of our transformation, what is termed by Kathleen Singh as a transpersonal awareness, our modified sense of *being* begins to encounter the collective. Our personal sense of self unfolds alongside the mythic, symbolic, religious and personal self. In all likelihood, those individuals that have returned from Near Death Experiences, NDEs, returned to human existence at this stage of transition. We come across many common elements of experience that occur for the individual during this process. The typical NDE involves a separation from body and sense-of-self as well as, a wider perspective of their surrounding environment. This can include remotely viewing loved ones, doctors and other relatives in the immediate vicinity. Another phase of this event involves the feeling of moving rapidly through a passage or tunnel. The individual has described encountering otherworldly spirits, religious symbols or friends and relatives. This stage of transition leads to an expanded sense of self, a sense of self experienced as far more than originally assumed. Our physical container we have called the body, mind and self, is suddenly insufficient and incapable of supporting its own consciousness.

What we may be experiencing in this stage of our evolution involves the disintegration of the personal ego and the unfolding of self into a larger state of *being*. Although only briefly discussed here, this process like the five-stages of death are disconcerting and often painful for the individual. The necessary abandonment of the known self most likely occurs with despair and loss. As an analogy, we can equate this emotional pain to a newborn's experience of teething. The infant is bewildered and startled by this necessary painful change and experience required for mortal life. Much like a new appendage, the sense of self is overwhelmed with this expansion and becomes the expansion as the final stage of this process. At this point, the concept of self-awareness is probably inadequate. If we equate the tadpole or caterpillar to the current sense of self, its radical transformation to an amphibian or butterfly may be analogous to the change of consciousness we undergo. During this final stage of transformation, the individual self becomes the ground of its own *being*. All prior resistance to relinquishing a separate sense of self disappears, and the profound realization that you are the *being* occurs. We also come to terms with the inner *I* of all things as the source, cause and reason for itself. Personal consciousness encounters its collective and possibly integrates *being* in the self as the self. This expansion as furthered described by Mrs. Singh is our returning to a more open, inclusive and expanded state of *being*. We begin to perceive the natural transformations in the world about us as the familiar and necessary. If we were to pay close attention to the current changes in our lives today, we can intuitively see that we are currently experiencing this return of self to its *being*. We can now ask what happens next, what happens to all that I have come to love, hate and admire about this personal me? Do we continue to live in some other place, location or time? As answered best in the words of Alan Watts, "We do not. We come to an end. But this is the end of the night."[14]

E. There is No Forever

Physical time is an illusion. As described By F.H. Bradley, time as an appearance contradicts itself and simply endeavors, unsuccessfully, to appear as an attribute of the timeless. The scientific term quantum entanglement, is the understanding that two widely separated systems can and do behave as if they were connected. This would be similar to you performing an action in New York, and another person simultaneously doing the exact same thing, as if in synchronization with you in Japan. Both individuals located in New York and Japan would have no physical connection with one another, but the actions would appear as if there was. Albert Einstein

---

14. Alan W. Watts, *Become What You Are,* (Boston, London: Shambhala Publications, 2003), p. 27.

referred to this as "spooky action at a distance". Scientists the world over are seeing that time is intrinsic to the specific object, and can only be perceived based on a reference to a larger clock or a world time. In this system of world time, humanity's temporal existence appears to track against a measured event of change. The basis for our belief that we exist in a reality where events occur on a regular basis or rhythmic pattern is due to material changes. What we do not fully comprehend is the complete inter-relationship between these objects, which represent the essence of an un-fragmented reality. Our current level of conscious awareness piece meals these changes together, and represents them as compartmentalized segments perceived as past, present and future. Reality cannot exists outside of itself or only be a part of itself. In George Santayana's book *Realms of Being,* he expresses this when he describes existence as having no medium or fixed conduit beyond itself. If we assume that an absolute space-time must exist, then we encounter a contradiction of looking for another reference through which *it* should flow.

What appears to us as a world of random events, gives rise to the premise that in its causality there must be an opposite or non-causal world. This is similar to the story of the three blindfolded men who each describe different parts of an elephant as different objects based on their limited sense of sight. Due to this same limitation of human consciousness, physical time on earth serves as a byproduct of a limited awareness, but is not an awareness of reality. We can say that it is conceptually difficult to imagine existence without a past, present and future. The difficulty rests in the fact that we do not approach this from the stance of unifying these three concepts as in a single relation. Within this process, we try to connect disparate events in a before and after fashion that appear as a series of phenomena related through or by time. If we examine this closely, we find that consciously and subconsciously we relate to each other from a personal unity of temporal arrangements. Our personal timelines or chronological arrangements match closely to one another to provide us the appearance of a common timeline.

Within the animal kingdom, we see numerous timelines that are very alien to ours. The lifespan of almost any animal, plant or insect shows us that existence does not require fixed moments that expands to the next in a sequential fashion. During late night dream or REM periods, humans often experience an accelerated time sequence of events. On waking reflection, we relate these dream periods as if they lasted longer than the obvious time our thinking consciousness can correlate. In essence, we exist in a world with numerous personal timelines constructed through a personal experience of change. Correlating changes or events merely allows us the ability to relate to one another in a mutual or common worldview. Although within our nightly dreams and imagination, our innermost conception of time is askew to our waking consciousness. In the next stage of our evolution what may appear to us in the *now* as the flux of time, may become the indissoluble moment. As described by the many great sages and thinkers of our past, a path to experience this unified self is always available to us. What we find in common in their descriptions of this state of mind, is a non-local awareness occurring outside of our measured sequential timeframes.

What these thinkers have discovered was that to go beyond the limitation of personal timelines, our personal self required silencing. In relinquishing self-awareness, our personal timelines also disappeared. As experienced in the Zen tradition called *zazen* or just sitting, physical time appears as an objectified reality, a reality that holds no emotional or personal content. What these thinkers observed during their meditations, was that time is strictly a phenomenon relative to human perception. As an example, if our current consciousness became that of a different species, our time reference would become radically different. It would be relative to that of the lifespan of a dog or insect or tree. In these scenarios, time would not occur in passing seconds, minutes or hours but possibly track against something seasonally or something we currently do not perceive. All sequences of time or progression may also appear non-linear and may not be event driven at all! In the words and wisdom of F. H. Bradley we read:

"It is not hard to conceive a variety of time-series existing in the Absolute. . . the direction of each series, one can understand, may be relative to itself, and may have as such no meaning outside. . .Let us take for example, a scheme like this:"

a	b	c	d
b	a	d	c
t	d	a	b
d	c	b	a

"Here if you consider the contents, you may suppose the whole to be stationary. It contains partial views, but as a whole, it may be regarded as free from change and succession."[15]

In Mr. Bradley's example, one can assume that what he refers to as the *absolute* is that which requires no time-reference. An *absolute* state of *being* one-step removed from the object. He also refers us to what many ancient and modern texts call the observer or witness. In the next chapter, we will revisit the concept of timelessness as it relates to reality.

F. There is only love

There is only love, but our definition of the word and its meaning is misused or misunderstood. We need to expand on our understanding of this word in order to prepare us for the next chapter where we will approach the foundation of our *being*. Historically, love

15. F. H. Bradley, *Appearance and Reality,* (Glasgow: Oxford University Press, 1893), p. 185.

includes a variety of emotions and beliefs such as affection, religious love, metaphysical love, ethical, political and other emotive expressions. In general, our modern concept of love is mostly a measure of desirability. If we look at the origins of the word love, we find it is derived from the Germanic form of the Sanskrit word *Lubh,* which means desire. The Greek word *Eros* also refers to a more physical love equated to sexual desire, which when rephrased in modern lingo became the word erotic. As human beings, we embrace the concept of self-love, love of country, family, music, words and numerous other forms of expressionistic fondness. Overall, our emotional response to this word brings about an emergence of a higher self in, of, or through the object of our affection. What we have also come to learn is that love often desires or commands mutual reciprocity. As put in the words of Christ, to love thy neighbor as thyself. In this sense, love is something that transcends space and time. As described in the words of writer and philosopher Deepak Chopra:

"In spiritual terms falling in love is an opening, an
opportunity to step into the timeless and stay there."[16]

What we hear echoed in romantic love is that the lover's feel unified in thought, deed and action, which is often described as being *one* or interchangeable. We also commonly equate love as the physical act of sex. In this respect, we see that love actually serves as a manifesting force, a force that draws emotion into actual life. Simply put, if we take a deeper look at the qualities we have attributed to the meaning of the word love, we begin to see that life and existence is a reflection of this attractive, integrative and creative emotion. If we put our analytical glasses back on, we see that love allows us the ability to transcend the feelings of a separate self. In this regard, love allows us to experience timelessness. We also see

---

16. Deepak Chopra, *Path to Love,* (New York: Random House, Audiobooks, 1997), Written & read by Deepak Chopra, M.D. - Abridged Nonfiction - 2.3 hours.

the integrative power of love in healing. What many natural healers have expressed is that they must become one with the individual who is ill in order to provide healing. It is through love this unification occurs. In Doctor Larry Dossey's words we read:

> "A major difference is that the unity that the healer feels with the patient is infused and transformed by love and caring. This is an essential factor whose importance simply cannot be overestimated. Healers experience a sense of holiness with that of wholeness, such that the universe seems Godlike, enchanted, and filled with love."[17]

We also read how non-judgmental love or unconditional love occurs when the ego or persona does not participate. Love allows one to empathize or assume the other's view as if they were this other person! In this sense, love and caring provides us the ability to emotionally and mentally become the other person, and in doing so, experience the other's reality as if it was our own. In experiencing this other as self, we also find that love now serves as a conduit of knowledge. The simple knowing of things, events and states of mind, become intuitively available for the individual when love transcends differences. Love shows us how interconnected and interdependent everyone and everything is. Far beyond the everyday use of the word and its connotation, love reflects the gratitude of inclusiveness, as the wholeness of self and the complimentary relationship of the natural world. We also learn that love helps us to experience a sense of acceptance and gratitude that empowers us to work through difficult or problematic events in our lives. Through acceptance and gratitude, a mutual self-disclosure also occurs. We create a "bond of trust" essential to the kind of intimacy that is characteristic of intimate relationships. This opens us up to experience a unity and solidarity with something or someone that at one point

17. Larry Dossey, *Recovering the Soul,* (New York: Bantam Books, 1989), p. 70.

appeared at a distance. Love and gratitude becomes a reciprocal sense of reality, not in the simple sense of giving and receiving, but in the awareness of one of the most basic reality's we possess as a complete *being*.

Putting our analytical glasses back on, we can begin to see that love in a broader sense, is more than the emotional response commonly attributed to the word. If we look at all the implications of the word we have discussed so far, we see that it is the force or energy allowing us the transformation of life beyond a time-based consciousness. In essence, love serves as the vehicle or doorway in becoming what we cannot perceive with the intellect or physical senses. This becoming or creation of *being* requires the capacity of unconditional love. Thinkers, prophets and sages throughout the ages stressed the importance of unconditional love. There is nothing sentimental or trite about the broader meaning behind love. Our misunderstanding of what love is, and its role in our day-to-day lives, has limited humanity in experiencing and utilizing our true nature. In this modern physical world of relative sciences and daily practicalities, it is disheartening to see that this one tangible reality has been so sorely misunderstood.

In this section of the book, we have laid the necessary groundwork to approach our next and more difficult area of discussion. Our "New Rules" touched on many areas as it related to understanding a clearer perspective of our reality. In trying to bring these new concepts together in a cohesive way, we now need to venture forward and discuss reality from these new perceptions. To help us begin, I would like to quote a short section of the Katha Upanishads translated by Eknath Easwaran in his book *Dialogue with Death*:

"The wise, realizing through meditation
The timeless, divine Self, so hard to see,
Hidden in the secret cave of the heart,
Leave pleasure and pain far behind.
The man who knows he is the subtle Self

Finds the source of all joy and lives in joy
Abiding, I see the gates of joy
Are opening for you, ..."[18]

Let us attempt to open the door to all possibilities in our search towards a better understanding of reality.

---

18. Eknath Easwaran, *Dialogue with Death*, (California: Nilgiri Press, 1981), p. 238.

3
Strictly Business

"Reality is the beginning not the end,
Naked Alpha, not the hierophant Omega,
Of dense investiture, with luminous vassals."
— Wallace Stevens

In our last chapter, we discussed new ways of looking at the world we perceive as well as ourselves. One can rightly say that the conclusions we have drawn has taken us to a far country! We have presented our reality as a single unified *being,* and the individual self as a passing phenomenon. In keeping with this chapter's title, we will now endeavor to describe this misunderstood *being,* you, along these new lines of inquiry. In order to set about this task, let us define the following guidelines to assist us:

- All natural events must remain equal in magnitude.
- No religious, orthodox or unorthodox beliefs can be used as a given.
- Popularity of an idea does not validate the idea.
- All possibilities in lieu of space constraints are open for discussion.
- And, if we cannot answer any specific question within the framework of our analysis, we must simply state it as an unknown.

On Being the Being

Working from the above criteria, the reader may raise the question of where do we begin? We can begin by confronting the basic question on the definition of existence. We have focused on existence as a contingent quality, an event that enters into or is *being,* and eventually terminates into non-*being.* Based on our above guidelines, we must look at this line of logic as it relates to human consciousness. To begin, the individual has first perceived content of the world as its own consciousness and everything else as object to it. These objects and other consciousnesses are separate entities often discerned as self-aware *beings* alike ourselves. In essence, here is the problem we encounter with another's existence, in the face of the sudden realization of this other, we jump to the conclusion there exists something that we are *not.* It is this *not,* which is the final step our consciousness makes prior to encountering the wider concept of nothingness. This is what the other has lucidly presented us with all along, existence vs. non-existence. This knowledge is our individual perception of self, represented as a difference or tension within life's framework. The fact of our own mortality is not in question. What is in question is the need to define an absolute something or an absolute nothing. Let us begin to describe this nothingness as an absolute non-existence, and this something as an absolute existence. Conceptually, to attempt to define nothingness is enigmatic at best, but we can approach this subject by utilizing the concept of *space,* or the empty matter between objects. The philosopher Immanuel Kant assists us by outlining the following criteria:

1. Space is not an empirical concept, abstracted from other experiences, for space is presupposed in referring sensations to something external, and external experience is only possible through the presentation of space.

2. Space is a necessary presentation a priori, which underlies all

external perceptions, for we cannot imagine that there should be no space, although we can imagine that there should be nothing in space.[1]

In Kant's first quote above, he makes it clear that all perception is dependent on a foreknowledge that objects exist in the background of space and distance. In both of his points, all of our physical surroundings are dependent on a non-physical medium in order for perception to occur. This non-physical or non-local medium called space or the void between objects is the nothingness we now define. We can also say that physical objects appear to originate through the void as supernatural incongruities. Taking this thought further, we can begin to understand that physical objects do not originate from this nothingness, but are a part of it. Regardless of our considerations on the relationship between what is existence vs. non-existence, we can say that nothingness in context allows perception. In essence, we come face to face with the realization that the inapprehensibility of nothingness brought on by the other's presence is a requirement for consciousness to exist. Similarly, when mutually perceived by the *other*, we must conclude that nothingness is a contextual given. In essence, we manifest our concrete foundation or reality as a fundamental given. The problem with fundamental givens as objected to in our above criteria is our inability to come to terms with, or define our casual existence.

Better stated, we cannot resolve a *given* such as a conceptual nothingness or something-ness into an absolute understanding. We personify this conundrum by defining it with relative causal qualities such as up vs. down, left vs. right, us vs. other and so on. The perception of what appears as a plurality of consciousness creates the illusion of multiple existents. In perceiving this, we view the world as something that exists outside of what we define as *self*. The problem we encounter is that this *us* must eliminate itself from the perception by these self-same conclusions. What we are expe-

---

1. Kant, *Physics & Philosophy-World Perspectives*, (1958), p. 87.

riencing, is the dualism of what we can now term a local reality vs. a non-local reality. To understand what we define as non-local reality, we can say human awareness is the phenomena that can place itself within a non-physical state. Humanity currently does this by utilizing deep contemplation, meditation, simple daydreaming and visions. In this sense, consciousness exhibits no determinate locale or specific physicality. When daydreaming or in REM sleep, consciousness creates a non-physical reality which for the dreamer *IS* reality. In Larry Dossey's book *Recovering the Soul, a Scientific and Spiritual Search*, he expresses this when he writes:

> "There is something more that is essential to ourselves than the flimsy ego, and that whatever this essence is, it cannot be localized to a specific point in space and time."[2]

What we misunderstand as individuals, is that we perceive ourselves to be a local phenomenon in a physical body inhabiting the immediate now *and* a non-local reality. This paradox is quickly resolved when we understand that our *only* reality is not a local phenomena but a non-local one. Our time-space dependence in perceiving ourselves as a local reality has placed the individual psyche in an emotional straightjacket. In Alan Watts' book *This is It*, he comments on this by describing consciousness as a cosmic or universal event. He further explains that from a cosmic understanding, we find release from the limitation of a focused self-consciousness. Our fixed beliefs, feelings and emotions when perceived as a local reality, create our worldviews. We also see many examples of non-local beliefs in our religious references and daily references. It is not surprising that modern science also speaks of reality as that of a non-local dimension. In Fred Alan Wolf's book *Parallel Universes*, he writes:

---

2. Larry Dossey, *Recovering the Soul*, (New York: Bantam Books, 1989), p. 49.

"Knowledge of a single event, isolated from all other events, is no knowledge at all. Knowledge without a sense of the past and an anticipation of the future is no knowledge at all. In brief, single data points without any reference to the future or the past are not even recorded data. They simply do not exist."[3]

Regardless of this knowledge, humanity in general believes that we are dependent and supported by a non-local *being* without physical form or time dependence. This dualistic belief has hampered our coming to terms with our own natural state of being a non-local *entity*. What is also confusing is that we perceive ourselves to exist in a physical world that adheres to the laws of both local and non-local realities. Let us look at what our scientists have discovered concerning our physical world. In 1964, J. S. Bell published his theory called Bell's Theorem. Bell's Theorem mathematically described the concept of subatomic particles connected in ways that transcends space and time. In essence, he stated that anything that happens to one particle of matter affects all other particles. This effect was described as immediate or superluminal. Bell's theory, which describes reality as non-local is remarkable for several reasons:

1. It is a mathematical proof, not a conjecture or speculation.
2. It is a proof about reality not appearances and,
3. It is counter-intuitive: everywhere local facts are dependent on a non-local reality.

This instantaneous connectedness works from one particle to another and for the universe on a whole. Another scientific pioneer by the name of Rupert Sheldrake also described this in his theory of Morphogenetic Fields. Sheldrake proposed that all material systems remain organized by known energy and material factors as well as, unseen organizing fields. This also implied that whenever one mem-

---

3. Fred Alan Wolf, *Parallel Universes*, (New York: Touchtone Books, 1990), p. 307.

ber of a species learns a new behavior, the causative field for that mind-set is changed. If a new behavior is sufficiently repeated, that behavior will resonate and affect the entire species. These scientific thoughts also fit comfortably with Carl Jung's Collective Consciousness theory. If we look at the many species in nature, we see their evolution or change occurs towards greater adaptability within their environment. What does not seem obvious to us as observers, is the continuous evolution of the mind in the area of awareness and its perceptions. Teilhard de Chardin, a Jesuit priest and philosopher, described a concept called the Omega Point. For Teilhard, this Omega Point represented a universal fulcrum of synthesis or integration towards singularity. This singularity allowed for a reconciliation of the individual ego with what he termed the metaphorical *all*. He further stated that beyond being an evolving species, we are active participants in the evolution process. This participation was not an external phenomenon reduced to its parts, but rather *evolution* becoming conscious. In Teilhard's book, *The Phenomenon of Man*, he outlined a "threefold synthesis" of the material and physical world with the world of mind and spirit. This he described as the past within the future and the many with the one. In essence, Teilhard's theory allows for a vision in which the Universal and the Personal self are reconciled. For Teilhard the cosmos was not an impersonal place but instead Hyper-Personal. His view posits humanity as an integral facet of nature, and not an external phenomenon subject to the whims of an external *being* or force.

Similarly, we see these views reflected in Dr. Wayne Dyers' description of humanity as that of an environorganism, nature as ones' extended body. These conclusions draw us closer to the understanding that as a perceived *us* or individual, we have limited our perception to a day-to-day existence. The question now asked is how does the individual experience itself at this larger level of awareness? Aldous Huxley, a well-known British writer, expressed this best when he wrote that each of us is capable of mentally experiencing everything happening everywhere in the universe. What he felt was that our brain or nervous system acted as a massive filter of events to prevent us from experiencing a sensory overload. He called this potential in us our *Mind at Large*. This is also similar to Irwin Schrodinger's view on the mind and its capacity. Both men conjectured that the mind and the physical world are co-evolving. This unity of mind as Schrodinger described is not a piecemeal event divided up in its bits and pieces, but as radical as it may sound, is the complete *all*. In Schrodinger's words:

"... inconceivable as it seems to ordinary reason, you
– and all other conscious beings as such are all in all.
Hence this life of yours which you are living is not
merely a piece of the entire universe, but is, in a certain
sense, the whole only this whole is not so constituted that
it can be surveyed in one glance."[4]

Additionally, Meister Eckhart a German mystic of the thirteenth century also spoke of this wholeness of mind when he wrote:

"When a man goes out of himself to find or fetch God,
he is wrong. I do not find God outside of myself nor
conceive him excepting as my own and me. . . And the
manner of our knowing shall be this, I him as he me, not
more or less, just the same."[5]

Each of us existing as the whole makes sense when we take into account the many thoughts and scientific theories these writers have provided us. Our inability to see beyond this logical or split minded perspective is reminiscent of the story of the three blindfolded sages that touch various parts of an elephant's body. Each sage mistakes the elephant for something else; its tail for a rope, its trunk for a

4. Erwin Schrodinger, *My View of the World*, (Connecticut: Ox Bow Press, 1983), p. 22.
5. Meister Eckhart, *Eckhart I*, quoted in J. M. Cohen and J-F. Phipps, *The Common Experience*, (New York: St. Martin's Press, 1979) p. 112.

snake and its leg for a tree stump. With the removal of their blindfold the full picture snaps into focus and the breadth of what they are experiencing becomes obvious. The removal of this blindfold as described by Alan Watts is the relinquishment of self-consciousness towards what he terms Cosmic Consciousness. This Cosmic Consciousness does not imply the dissolution of self or sense of self, but rather the illumination of a perspective towards a truer sense of *being*. As a non-local *being*, we exist as the full awareness of all within all. Throughout time, humanity has mistaken its connectivity of self and non-local reality as illusionary. The philosophy of Jainism and Buddhism also speak of this blindfold as bondage of the physiognomy. With the removal of this blindfold, a psychological step towards one's enlightenment is perceivable.

Although the mystics and scientists world over have encountered this non-local sense of *being*, there still remains much fear or simple ignorance over our intrinsic nature. This wariness or fear of self, as described by Michael Talbot in his book *The Holographic Universe,* is due to our ingrained belief that time and space are the irrefutable realms of our existence. Mr. Talbot describes the reasoning behind our conditioning as follows:

> "Although we are taught that we "think" with our brains, this is not always true. Under the right circumstances our consciousness—the thinking, perceiving part of us— can detach from the physical body and exist just about anywhere it wants to."[6]

The view Mr. Talbot presents us with sounds difficult if not impossible to believe. Understanding that time and space has served humanity in interacting with what we term the physical world, it is hard if not impossible to imagine a reality without both. In an attempt to understand or conceptualize this, we must revisit our current perceptions of

6. Michael Talbot, *The Holographic Universe*, (New York: HarperCollins Publisher, 1991), p. 234.

both time and space.

Science has historically considered time as a basic requirement for human existence without exception or question. If we attempt to envision existence without time, we immediately confront the issue of location, or that of existing in space at a specific point. We can understand this concept of non-location by using the analogy of dreaming. When we are dreaming, our consciousness exists as the characters, places and events within the dreaming mind. If for instance we are visiting a remote location such as a childhood home or neighborhood in the dream state, the people and places in the dream we believe are separate and distinct entities from us. On waking, the individual quickly discerns that all the dream material was in the mind of the self. The events in our dream life exist for us emotionally, but are not local events that occur in conscious reality. From a psychological basis, non-localism is an unmediated action or reaction that requires no space or time as its constraint. It is easy to deny its existence because it does not seem to make sense. Nevertheless, and as in our example above, when we are dreaming we experience non-local reality and exist as all facets of the dream environment. In essence, we reside in multiple dimensions that interrelate and coincide in the most intricate arrangement of agreements. Indeed, this may be the only way we can exist at all, our *being* assuming possession of all artifacts in our environment as we do in our dreaming worlds.

Physicist Fred Hoyle believed that these many dimensions overlay each other in our dream life and in our waking life. When we participate in a specific mode of awareness, we tune in to a specific sense of self or identity, with all other externalized events perceived as existing as separate events from *us*. Yet, when the dreamer wakes, it is clearly understood that the dream specifics; people, places, and events, where solely owned and created by them. Additionally, within our dreaming state remote or non-linear information is available to us instantaneously. In his book *Parallel Universes,* Fred Alan Wolf helps us understand why our waking consciousness does not experience this phenomenon. He states that our minds cannot handle the complexity of what he calls 'interference' from these many realities. Conscious thought, unable to resolve this integrated unity, attempts to break it down into separate singular events against the backdrop of an imagined stable reference we call space and time.

As we move away from the illusory nature of our tuned in reality or waking consciousness, we encounter a major problem in understanding non-local-reality. The problem we are facing is if our true state of existence is that of a non-local existence, then where are we now? Throughout the ages and in the many languages and metaphors of the mystics and spiritual teachers, this question required answering. In the Mahayana school of thought and in many Vedantic writings, we find that all external events, experiences and pursuits are merely phenomenal and possess no intrinsic reality. According to these teachings, even our thoughts were merely devices, and a distraction from the realization of our true *being*. Similarly, in the Asian Consciousness-Only Doctrine, we come across the belief of the non-existence of the individual *self*. Within this doctrine, reality is merely a construction based on wrong ideas, and the existence of a *self* is an impossible concept. In reading through a number of these teachings, we repetitively come across the thought that we as physical beings simply do not exist! From a Western viewpoint, the connotation of a loss of self is a negative statement or an absurdity based on an ingrained cultural sense of individuality. Yet, if we read past and present European philosophers, we hear these same statements echoed in their writings. In the Kantian school of thought, we encounter the thought that there are no such objects immanent in our experience and that we are intimately involved in an illusion. Similarly, Hegelian thought presents us with the concept that *being* means *being* for consciousness, and that the universe is nothing but the content of consciousness. Also echoed in the words and writing of the Dalai Lama we hear:

"Realize that the body is impermanent like a clay vessel.
Know that the phenomena are without inherent existence,
like mirages."[7]

Our belief in the existence of objects and the habit of supposing their independent existence does not hold its basis in reason or logic. Belief in the coherence and continuity of objects alleviates us from the fear of the aging process and change. For many individuals, life is a multitude of workable stable patterns in consciousness. These workable stable patterns represent the self's attempts to justify its own existence. As stated in the words of Jean-Paul Sartre:

". . . we discovered consciousness as an appeal to *being* . . .
the cogito refers immediately to a being-in-itself which is
the object of consciousness."[8]

The implications both from a metaphysical and philosophical perspective are staggering. The paradox presented is that our existence, or individual self is only a reference to *being*, and the justification for itself is its goal. To help us down this path, we can begin to look at consciousness as an interrogative tool like that of a flashlight or stethoscope. When we use this flashlight or stethoscope in our daily experience, we quickly recognize the self's limitation and its inability to reveal more than a disjointed picture of the entire view. We encounter the object apart from its myriad of other connecting situations. In the case of the stethoscope, we separate out the patient's heartbeat from the patient. The confusion of perception in waking consciousness is that it can never completely embrace reality in its larger context. Based on this, humanity rationalizes its existence or understanding of reality as a subset of meanings and compartmentalized external events. The self or cause for its

---

7. Dalai Lama, *Advice on Dying*, (New York: Atria Books, 2002), p. 159.
8. Jean-Paul Sartre, *Being and Nothingness*, (New York: Philosophical Library, 1956), p. 785.

existence becomes a moving question defined by its motion. One can say that the age-old question of which came first, the chicken or the egg, is not a question requiring resolution, but rather the tenable position of our current reality.

From a casual world perspective, it can quickly be seen that all that exists can only be defined by its absence or compliment e.g. cold vs. hot, up vs. down, right vs. left vs. right etc . . . What is intrinsic to everything alive and breathing is an existence whose underpinnings are based on a conceptual nothingness. Martin Heidegger, a well-known philosopher, emphasized the opposites in which *being* and non-*being* must relate to each other. His thought was that our reality is the tension resulting from these two concepts, and this tension the cause of the apparent *self*. If we can begin to look at the concept of nothingness without the negative mindset embedded in our present understanding, we can begin to see the absolute balance in this. Jean Paul Sartre helps us with this by writing:

"It is in nothingness alone that being can be surpassed. At the same time it is from this point of view of beyond the world that being is organized into the world, which means on the one hand that human reality rises up as an emergence of being in non-being and on the other hand that the world is "suspended" in nothingness."[9]

Maybe this is what Siddhārtha Gautama, the founder of Buddhism, meant when he declared:

"There is, Oh Monks, a not-born, a not-become, a not-made, a not-compounded. Monks, if that unborn, not-become, not-made, not-compounded were not, there would be no escape from this here that is born, become, made and compounded."[10]

---

9. Ibid., pp. 786-787.
10. Buddha, *The Udana*, Chapter 8 Section 3.

In essence, that tree, book, mountain and your sense of being are the creator of the outline, object and its absence. The implication of this as quoted by Siddhārtha, is that our sense of reality without its absence would limit us to a reality of an indescribably confining nature. Let us look at what it means to have free will as conscious individuals.

Can we argue whether humanity has free will or is destined to act and respond based on casual relationships, pre-destinations or random events? If we place our dependence on a state of non-*being,* we open the door to understand this enigmatic entity, you, along the lines of self-determination. What humanity defines as god would need to possess the innate ability of self-creation and self-annihilation for its complete freedom. Human consciousness peering over the edge of these enormous concepts rejects the view and mistakenly externalizes the subject. What we misunderstand is that the owner of the view is one's own consciousness, and what precedes all action is its conception unrealized. As difficult as it might seem, consciousness embraces non-consciousness or non-*being* in order to maintain its state of all possibilities. The minute there is a cognitive process or reflective behavior on the part of the individual, consciousness has to disassociate itself from the act of awareness. If you pay close attention to your internal thought process, you will notice that there is a moment of void occurring prior to thought formation or reflection.

Consciousness must embrace its own polar opposite in order to exist, and non-consciousness must be its conceptual partner. In the truest game of hide and seek, the reality of the self must be hidden within itself as a non-*being.* Alan Watts writes a beautiful description to this effect in his book called *The Book.* He describes the game god plays as that of hiding in a myriad of forms, and pretending to be you and everything around us. The ground rules of this game, is in the forgetting this game is in progress in order to insure it remains hidden. The confusion created by this game of hide and seek could be described as a social psychosis, or humanity's fear of ending the game. We find our understanding of freedom or independence as the choice of not recovering the self, and remaining at a distance from *being* and not *being*. This state or stance our *being* has created is the wonder and awe of reality we experience within life's situational states. In the *Astavakra Samhita* written around the fifth or fourth century BCE and ascribed to the sage Astavakra, he expresses this confusion and awe when we read:

> "Where is the self, or where the non-self, where is what
> is fair, auspicious, and virtuous, and where what is foul,
> inauspicious, and sinful, where is thinking-pondering-
> and-anxiety, and where is not-thinking, non-anxiety—for
> me who abide in my own glorious greatness."[11]

Our phenomenal world of experience cloaked in its mysteries, is the ego's attempt to reflect itself in its own mirror of self. The problem with the ego's attempt in trying to see itself as a *real* thing is that it frustrates itself into further conditioned existence. The ego's only recourse is to alleviate the dilemma of separation from its *being* through escapism.

Ironically, the non-*being* defined as nothingness, allows the non-local self to experience self from the widest possible perspective. It is not necessary to perceive *being* and non-*being* to understand freedom of choice, but we need to remain open to both conceptually. The very structure and floating process of humanity's psyche experienced as awareness, is the vehicle to its exclusion and its inclusion of both. What we call the transcendent state, referred to as bliss, Nirvana, Heaven, etc . . ., must vanish with the self. There is an Indian parable that describes our journey as that of an occupant in a boat with oars crossing a stretch of open sea. As we approach the distant shore, we come to realize that we have made the jour-

---

11. Quoted in Heinrich Zimmer's, *Philosophies of India*, (New York: Meridian, 1956), p. 451.

ney without oars and the boat itself was an illusion. Finally, we come to realize that there never was a journey, and even the remote shore never existed. This realization is not the despairing individual confused by sensory illusion rather, it is the awakened self to the realization of its *being* and non-*being*. The most enlightening and terrifying realization in coming to terms with our cultural or social sense of self, is that of non-existence. Modern humanity deeply rooted in the creator vs. creation epochs, necessitates the need for an individual ego for fear of its survival. What is misunderstood is that the greatest freedom of self is in the awareness that self is uninvolved or unconcerned with its own outcome or existence. In order to accomplish this displacement, *being* requires or assumes a non-positional state or existence in an endless variety of perspectives. *Being's* neutral position can be understood as the only means to experience freedom or reality. True freedom requires the distancing or elimination of all remnants of self. The hindrance of ego as expressed by the many scholars, theologians, scientists and philosophers, opens the debate on whether control of mind or matter is the power we have equated to a supreme *being*. Let us look at what we define as omnipotence and its relationship to humanity.

Humanity has historically attributed the unknown world to an awe-inspiring entity that through causal means, created the natural laws of our planet. What we see is humanity's transference of personal ego to that of a superego. By placing our personal selves as the primary power broker of reality, it seemed to make sense to attribute these same qualities to that of an ultimate power broker. Personification of divinity is no different than imagining a face of the moon. This superman, as written about by the philosopher Fredrich Nietzche, is nothing more than a bloated ego caught in its own absurdity. This was the dilemma the reader encountered with the title of the seventh chapter of this book *"My God, You are God"*, the immediate thought was that of an individual endowed with supernatural abilities, and placed in a position where it might lose itself in delusions of grandeur. In C. Trungpa's book *The Myth of*

On Being the Being

Freedom, he goes on to explain that the ego seems beautiful because we have unified its aggressive nature as that of the self. The ego has lost sight of its innate intelligence and then endeavors to rely on its forceful nature. The intelligence that Trungpa refers to is a natural awareness of the bondage the ego knowingly exerts on itself.

Through material goals and desires of all kinds including health, wealth and fame, the ego attempts to maintain the relationship of power broker to reality. It then farms out the big questions of life to a divine power broker who must subconsciously resemble us. We also encounter this perspective of ego's misguided need to be power broker to reality in the Chinese Book of Changes called the *I Ch'ing*. In the *I Ching*, we read that a universal balance is required in order to refine the mind of humanity. It further stresses that with the attainment of this 'mental transparency', one comes into direct contact with reality. The nurturing of this balanced reality is the *yin* and *yang*. In essence, the *yin* and *yang* protects one from becoming unbalanced and forgetting that the self can cause damage through distractions and human propensities. Some of these human propensities are present in the following hexagram of the *I Ch'ing* called Obstruction:

I Ch'ing – Hexagram 12

As a brief description of the above Hexagram, the top three solid lines represent the creative principle *yang*, and the second three broken lines represent the receptive principle *yin*. The two sets of three solid and broken lines on top of each other represent the two principles un-joined, which describe the obstruction. This implies that giving free reign to emotions, desires, impetuousness and other egoistic symptoms can cause false strength or power.

In essence, the ego has corrupted its own understanding of reality by exerting its relationship to the world as an aggressive entity. By interpreting power as an aggressive force, we have personified god as the ultimate master of aggressive forces in acts of creation and destruction. As expressed by the Indologist Heinrich Zimmer:

> "Only apparently is the universal substance implicated
> in this highest personal figure, which has been born, as
> a magnificent superego, out of a sublime state of godly
> consciousness-in-ignorance."[12]

This consciousness-in-ignorance as described by Zimmer is the delusion the personal ego feels in believing that it is a facet of this superego. Further, it envisions itself to be an aggressive force in some form of stunted adolescence. Based on humanity's limited understanding, the assumption we have made is that we are little gods in training. Little gods, that come closer to the superego of a fictitious god as we learn to exert more aggressive power. If we look at what the sages, philosophers and our own religious prophets have said, we learn that the true self is not an inflated ego or power broker of the causal world. They tell us that we have overlooked the anonymity of self as the source of sheer *being*, and our sense of self as the fundamental meaning of its own *being*. Our sense of *I* need not exert a force on itself or require proof of its existence. As expressed by Christ when approached by his disciples who wished to punish a township where they had encountered resistance, he responded:

> ". . . and they went, and entered into a village of the
> Samaritans to make ready for him. And they did not
> receive him, because his face was as though he would go
> to Jerusalem. And when his disciples James and John saw
> this, they said, "Lord, wilt thou that we command fire
> to come down from heaven, and consume them, even as

---

12 Heinrich Zimmer, *Philosophies of India*, (New York: Meridian, 1956), p. 425.

Elias did?" But he turned, and rebuked them, and said,
"Ye know not what manner of spirit ye are of. For the
Son of man is not come to destroy men's lives, but to
save them."[13]

His response exemplifies the nature of true self or *being* in its
innate state. Violent action and violent thought stands in the way of
the growth needed to lead us to reality. In this respect, indulging in
violence is doing to oneself what an enemy would wish done to you.
True *being* is a singularity that desires no force physically or emo-
tively. As expressed in the Buddhist text of the *Samyutta Nikaya,
Sutta III, 15* chapter and verse:

"Killing, you gain your killer.
Conquering, you gain one who will conquer you
insulting, insult   harassing, harassment.
And so, through the cycle of action, he who has
plundered gets plundered in turn."[14]

What we begin to learn from these passages is that our modern
beliefs in a power based divinity or omnipotent *being* is misguided.
In contrast to teleological reasoning, that of an ordered universe,
the philosopher David Hume also commented on the implication of
a necessary effect based on a regularity of events. Hume saw that
events are not separate but so intimately joined or interconnected
that they appear linear.

What both modern and past thinkers have realized, is that a casual effect is erroneous based on a misunderstood singularity. As
quoted in the above Sutta, "Killing, you gain / your killer," implies
not an effect derived from the act, but the act and its result as the

---

13. Jesus Christ, *The Bible* – King James Version, Luke chapter 9, verses 52-56.
14. *The Samyutta Nikaya*, is a Buddhist scripture, the third of the five nikayas or collections in the Sutta Pitaka, which is one of the "three baskets" that compose the Pali Tipitaka
of Theravada Buddhism. Sutta III, Chapter 15.

same. When seen from the perspective of a singular self, there is no such thing as a causal relationship, only the act for or against you by you exists. If we project this thought further, we can begin to see this interrelationship in detail as it relates to the world around us. If a mother sees her offspring playing in the busy thoroughfare of cars in the street, she inherently warns her child of the danger in doing so. No one would say she is psychic in knowing that the effect to her child could be disastrous. If we understand this from a level of deepened awareness, events that seem far-fetched or disconnected would become immediately obvious. This does not imply a form of telepathy or extra sensory perception rather it is simply seeing all events as a part of a single self. One can arguably ask whether the individual self can be experienced at such a large level of awareness, but we forget that on a completely automatic basis our bodies accomplish this feat daily. As expressed by the geneticist and scientist J. B. S. Haldane:

"Now, if the cooperation of some thousands of millions of cells in our brain can produce our consciousness, a true singularity, the idea becomes vastly more plausible that the cooperation of humanity, or some sections of it, may determine what Comte calls a Great Being."[15]

Auguste Comte referenced by Haldane in the above quote, lived a positivist philosophy and coined the word altruism. Altruism as defined by Comte was the need for individuals to help others and place their interests at the same level or priority. We see this same sentiment of "do unto others," expressed throughout history by the many enlightened thinkers. If we look carefully at what they are saying, it is not simply an expression of good deeds or moral acts, rather it is the keen awareness that we are a unified self and benefit

---

15. J. B. S. Haldane as quoted by W. David Kubiak, *The Big Body Problem*, paper delivered at the 3rd biennial Asia / Pacific Environmental NGO Forum, September 14, 1994, Kyoto, Japan.

from our own support. If we look at the psychology of unselfish behavior or cooperative altruism, we see all of nature working together in very intricate ways. As eloquently described by Richard Dawkins in his book *The God Delusion,* we understand this better when we read:

> "The bee needs nectar and the flower bees pollinating.
> Flowers can't fly so they pay bees in the currency
> of nectar, for the hire of their wings. Birds called
> honeyguiders can find bees' nests but can't break into
> them. Honey badgers (ratels) can break into bees'
> nests, but lack wings with which to search for them.
> Honeyguiders lead ratels (and sometimes men) to honey
> by a special enticing flight, used for no other purpose.
> Both sides benefit from the transaction."[16]

A complex interaction as described by Mr. Dawkins appears simple when we look at the individual moving about the natural world. Generally, no one would notice the complex interactions we undertake everyday as we wake in the morning, get dressed or move about our residence. It does not appear complex because on an automatic basis we see all our motions and interactions stemming from a connected undivided self. Similarly, if we could see the world or universe in this fashion, all events local and remote, would appear as an innate extension of our natural *being.* Again, let us remember the conclusions of Dr. Wayne Dyer's environorganism, the individual not perceived as a separate entity moving about the cosmos, but the cosmos itself. The brilliance and complexity of what we are is not fathomable as discrete objects of individuals or separate events. Our interconnected singularity *IS* the selfsame reality. Where then is the individual, that intimate self we have come to know, appreciate, love and at times despise? This is the topic of our next chapter and it is about this marvelous, enigmatic and beautiful creature, you.

16. Richard Dawkins, *The God Delusion,* (Boston: Houghton Mifflin, 2006), p. 217.

4

Your Magnificence

"How is it possible that a being with such sensitive jewels as the eyes, such enchanted instruments as the ears, and such a fabulous arabesque of nerves as the brain can experience itself as anything less than a god?"
—Alan Watts

You are magnificent!

In other words, you are magnificent.

As described in the words of Alan Watts quoted above, our bodies are a complex system that effortlessly carries on a staggering number of tasks day in and day out. Let us take a brief tour of this marvelous machine before we begin our discussion on humanity. Our bodies use many systems that work side by side including bones, blood vessels, nerves, muscles, heart, livers and others. The body contains more than 650 individual muscles attached to our skeleton, which provides the pulling power for us to move. The muscular system consists of three different types of muscle tissues: skeletal, cardiac and smooth. Each of these different tissues has the ability to contract or expand when needed. There are two types of muscles within our systems, these are the involuntary and voluntary muscles. Involuntary muscles appear to be automatically functioning, and voluntary muscles function after conscious deliberation. All of this allows the human body to move effortlessly like a well-oiled machine.

On Being the Being

The Skeletal System is composed of all your bones, ligaments, tendons, and acts as a protective device for your organs. They serve as a firm base for the attachments of all of our muscles. Without bones, your muscles would not function properly. Our body's circulatory system has three distinct parts; pulmonary circulation (The Lungs), coronary circulation (The Heart) and systemic circulation. Each of these parts must be working independently in order for all of them to work together. On average, our body has approximately five liters of blood continually traveling through it by way of the circulatory system. The heart, the lungs and the blood vessels work together to form the circulatory system. Your heart pumps and forces the blood on its journey throughout your body. The nervous system is responsible for sending, receiving and processing nerve impulses throughout the entire body. All of the organs and muscles inside our bodies rely on these nerve impulses to function, which literally serves as the master control unit. The brain and the spinal cord make up the central nervous system, which provides the body with information about its environment. These networks receive information by means of the five senses: sight, hearing, smell, taste and touch.

Although we can effortlessly continue this nonprofessionals' discussion of the human body, we would only scratch the surface of its many intricate parts and functions. The point of our effort here has been to emphasize the massive coordinated effort used in maintaining the human animal. Scientists and doctors have gathered tremendous data on the physical aspect of our existence, but what is missing here is that we can only rudimentarily speculate on the mind-body connection that completes this you. For us to understand this space-time event called humanity, we will need to take a painfully eye-opening journey into our physiological and psycho-evolutionary makeup. The physical evolutionary ladder of humanity began 5-10 million years ago. Our species called the *Hominid* refers to the human animal whose species grew from the primate family of apes. Walking on two legs as opposed to on all four limbs was required due to the loss of forest and jungle. The need to survey longer stretches of grasslands to avoid predators, required sight from a standing position. Scientists speculate that the beginning of our line of evolution is the species called *Australopithecus Ramidus,* which lived about 4.4 millions years ago. Discovered through fossil records, this species of humanity was still very ape-like in posture and lifestyle. From a social lifestyle, we can assume these individuals moved in small groups of fifteen to thirty members as primate groups of today do.

From a psychological perspective, a group this size is managed by an Alpha member. This Alpha member would likely be a male whose intentions where visually signaled to the group for tasks such as migration, feeding, mating and group cohesiveness. Consciousness at this stage would be strictly instinctual in the sense that the natural world is lived through reactive behaviors and immediate group needs. Contents of the mind would be limited to casual events, and the Alpha Male of the group would need to be visually present in order to insure group cohesiveness. What is critical to note here is that this group of *Hominids* like the *Australopithecus* that followed a million years or so later, consisted of a group of likely twenty or thirty members. This limited number of members was a critical factor in insuring the immediate visual cueing, maintenance and cohesiveness of the entire group mind. Self-consciousness during this phase of evolution can be seen as non-existent as it relates to in-depth reflective or analytical ability.

If we move forward through time about 2.3 million years, we encounter *Homo habilis* commonly referred to as the Handy Man. These fossils first discovered by Mary and Louis Leakey in Tanzania, had remains that included primitive stone tools. With this species, we see greater intelligence and social organization similar to that of modern chimpanzees. *Homo habilis* is the ancestor of the more sophisticated *Homo ergaster*, which in turn gave rise to the more modern human-appearing species *Homo erectus*. Again, we see an enlarged ability towards tool usage and further social skills such as shelter building and burial. Within this line of evolution, we see the emergence of *Homo antecessor,* which existed about 800,000 years ago and possessed facial characteristics closer to the modern humans. *Homo heidelbergensis* appeared about 500,000 years ago with more advanced tooling, and around 130,000 years ago we see the arrival of *Homo neanderthalensis.* With the remains of *neanderthalensis,* scientists have found over 60 types of tools engraved with animal symbols. The current species of humanity is *Homo sapien.* Throughout these stages of evolution, we also encounter an increase in the size of the cranium (brain case) and group size. In the words of Anthropologist R.I.M Dunbar:

> "To maintain the stability of the large groups
> characteristic of humans by grooming alone would place
> intolerable demands on time budgets. It is suggested that
> (1) the evolution of large groups in the human lineage
> depended on the development of a more efficient method
> for time-sharing the processes of social bonding and that
> (2) language uniquely fulfills this requirement. . . . It
> is suggested that language evolved to allow individuals
> to learn about the behavioral characteristics of other
> group members more rapidly than is possible by direct
> observation alone."[1] [1]

What Mr. Dunbar is suggesting in the above quote is that group size and improved social dynamics, required additional support systems such as rudimentary language. The simple ability of visually informing a group member becomes less available as the size of the group increases. Unless the Alpha Male could be in a hundred places at the same time, he would be unable to maintain group cohesiveness. How then do the larger groups form and remain cohesive over time?

---

1. R. I. M. Dunbar, *Co-Evolution of Neocortex Size, Group Size and Language in Humans*, Human Evolutionary Biology Research Group, (London: University College London, 1993).

To answer this we need to turn our attention to the psycholog-ical-evolutionary aspects of our early ancestors with an emphasis on their ability to communicate. As primitive societies grew further into tribes of hundreds and larger, group cohesiveness becomes a larger problem. The assumption we have made is that these early humans had the aid of conscious awareness to deliberate on these changes, and correspondingly work together in these larger groups. Through the millions of years of physical evolution described above, we have left out the fact that self-consciousness slowly and at times painfully evolved. As an aid in our search to understand the evolution of consciousness, we can use the following chart placing our physical evolution alongside our mental evolution:

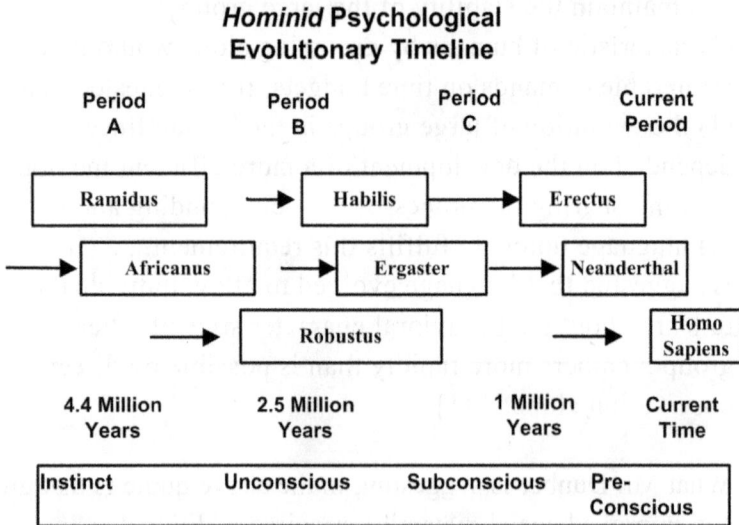

**Hominid Psychological
Evolutionary Timeline**

Period A	Period B	Period C	Current Period
Ramidus	Habilis	Erectus	
Africanus	Ergaster	Neanderthal	
	Robustus		Homo Sapiens
4.4 Million Years	2.5 Million Years	1 Million Years	Current Time
Instinct	Unconscious	Subconscious	Pre-Conscious

If we look at Period A in the above timeline, we can see early humans of 4.4 million years ago based on current level of conscious awareness, may not have been a conscious or self-aware species. These ancestors likely lived with what might be termed an intuitive instinct with strong environmental behaviors. During Period B of our timeline, we can say that humanity's environment is primarily that of tool use and learned behaviors. Nevertheless, we still do not encounter reflective or conscious behavior. Our graphic distinctions of humanity's conscious evolution like our model above overlap across extended time. As an example, during Period B through C we see the inklings of reflective behavior likely due to the need for the Alpha Leader to project group intentions. These initial intentions expand during Period C over the last 100,000 years as the emergence of primitive language takes shape. Unlike many species, humanity possesses a well-developed voice box that allows for the rendering of complex sounds necessary for speech. With this small physical advance, the ability to convey group or tribal intentions expands dramatically. Although still in its infancy, internal group members can now signal each other to warn of dangers at a distance. The Alpha Male or group leader becomes the sound of his utterances, and his vocal intentions are projected. What this implies is that instinct starts it harrowing journey to learned behaviors and auditory recollection. This auditory recollection serves the group to obey the Alpha Male's commands as its relative size grows. As expressed in the words of anthropologist Julian Jaynes:

> "When dominant individuals give a warning cry or run, others of the group flee without looking for the source of danger. It is thus the experience of one individual and his dominance that is an advantage to the whole group."[2]

During the ensuing 100,000 years, the group size grows and language or signaling expands. Can we assume self-awareness or reflective behaviors are occurring during this time? Unfortunately, any metric needed to assume this is unavailable to us. What we have during this time is mostly fossil records that speak to the physiological aspects of early humans and group dynamics. Fortunately, this primitive form of language expands over the years and becomes the eventual symbolic forms of written language. As poignantly expressed in the words of Owen Barfield:

---

2. Julian Jaynes, *The Origin Of Consness in the Break-down of the Bicameral Mind*, (Boston: Houghton Mifflin Company, 1977), p. 127.

"Languages, considered historically, bear within themselves a record of the evolution of human consciousness."[3]

From here, we can condense our timeline as it relates to the written word as follows:

Hominid Psychological Evolutionary Timeline

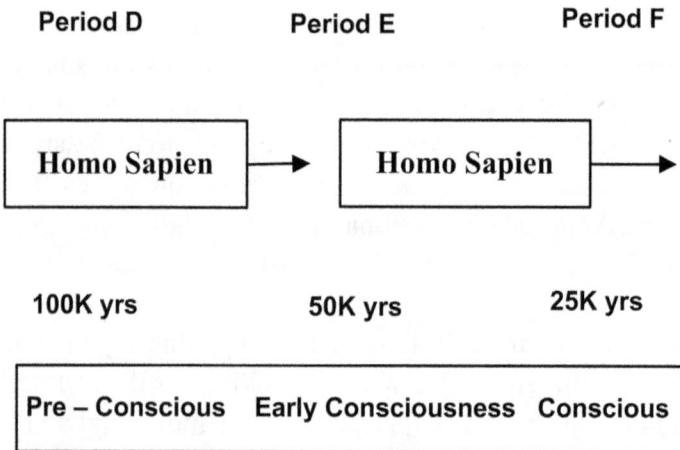

Period D	Period E	Period F

Homo Sapien	→	Homo Sapien	→

100K yrs	50K yrs	25K yrs

Pre – Conscious	Early Consciousness	Conscious

The group dynamic during period D and E has now becomes that of the city or town dynamic were hundreds of members now reside. How has consciousness evolved during this time? In an attempt to define consciousness, we can say that it is a subjective state requiring more than the physical presence of a self or individual. Further defined in the words of physicist Danah Zohar we read:

"The unity of our conscious experience, the thread of focused attention that draws together the myriad sensory impressions, underlies all other features of that

---

3. Barfield, *The Origin and Development of Language*, (London: Poetic Diction, 1928), Quoted Section.

experience. Like the notes of a melody or the many separate features of apples or more general visual scenes, the content of our consciousness hang together. They form a whole, a "picture." Each part of that whole derives its meaning from the whole and in its own being reflects both the whole and all its other constituent parts."[4]

What we need to take into account here is that evolution is a hard taskmaster. By no means did humanity's transition to self-consciousness come easily or effortlessly. More than likely early humans continued to rely heavily on visual stimuli like their ancestors, and these abilities augmented with rudimentary language. The transition from visual behavior patterns to language or symbolic behaviors could not have been easy. We might ask what this period of existence was like for early humanity. Again, in the words of Anthropologist Julian Jaynes:

"The most plausible hypothesis is that verbal hallucinations were a side effect of language comprehension which evolved by natural selection as a method of behavioral control."[5]

In other words, our ancestors in their long rise to consciousness heard and imagined voices. In modern psychology, we would diagnose this condition as schizophrenia. As difficult as it is to imagine, the transition towards our current level of consciousness involved visual hallucinations, auditory hallucinations (voices) and probably a host of disturbing associations. Early humanity would be at a loss to understand this new psychic change brought on with the advent of more complex modes of communication. Here we note

---

4. Danah Zohar, *The Quantum Self*, (New York: William Morrow, 1990), p. 69.
5. Julian Jaynes, *The Origin of Consciousness in the Break-down of the Bicameral Mind*, (Boston: Houghton Mifflin Company, 1977), p. 134.

two effects of language on early humanity, that of the psychological change towards consciousness, and its effect (voices) as a means for behavioral control and group ordering. We can all attest to the fact that during stressful periods of our modern lives, we can hear the voices of others within ourselves and recall their words and advice. Looking again at group dynamics during Period F of our chart, we would see language evolving as modifications of intentional calls and commands to the group. Vocabulary would be that of a variation of sounds, these sounds elicited by the Alpha Leader in order to maintain group cohesion. Group control during this early rise to consciousness was probably due to, and I would stress the word *probably*, a less conscious individual obeying the group leader or king. Here we encounter the concept of a voice one hears and obeys with all its supernatural connotations. As eloquently expressed by Julian Jaynes:

> "This was the paradigm of what was to happen in the next eight millennia. The king dead is a living god."[6]

He further goes on to express that the king's tomb, our previous Alpha Group Leader is treated with reverence as the authoritarian voice still echoing in the minds of his tribe. The reader may ask, what caused these voices or this altered reality? Here we can begin to tie in the physical evolution of humanity with this psychological change.

The capacity and need for increased environmental control is nowhere more striking than in our species. Humanity in increasing its ability to control the environment required that the physical brain evolve and react to sensory information on a larger scale. This expansion or need for further brain evolution required utilizing distinct regions of the brain. In essence, the human brain consists of four principal parts: the brain stem (*diencephalons* consisting of the *thalamus* and *hypothalamus*) the *cerebrum* and *cerebellum*. Found

---

6. Ibid., p. 143.

in the upper area directly beneath the top of the skull, the *cerebrum* is the largest part of the brain. The surface area of the *cerebrum* is the *cerebral cortex* or *neo-cortex,* where billions of neurons are contained. On an evolutionary scale of time, this is the most recently evolved or developed area of the human brain. Although early brain structure or size does not allude to an abnormal functioning of brain, we nevertheless see a particular pattern of behavior in cases of frontal lobe damage in modern clinical cases. How would these individuals appear to us and behave in a modern world? Using the mental illness of schizophrenia as a clue, in the words of William Calvin we read:

> "The schizophrenics with negative symptoms are the ones likely to suffer from frontal lobe disorder. These people are drastically slowed down in their thought and speech, have blunted emotions. They seem unable to express empathy with others, and their attention spans may be shortened."[7]

Viewing this on a more reactive basis, he writes:

> "They hallucinate, seeing things that aren't there.
> They may have delusions, thinking that God is out to punish them. Some have bizarre behaviors or thought disorders."[8]

Again, we are only commenting on the closest parallel to what early humans might have experienced as a general mode of thought and perception. Early humanity, in tapping into this region of the brain, encountered what we can call the side effects of a much larger appendage. As an analogy, it would be similar to a child suddenly placed on a large airplane unaware of its size and magnitude, and

---

7. H. Calvin, *The Cerebral Symphony*, (New York: Bantam Books, 1989), p. 62.
8. 8. Ibid., p.62.

not given the instruction on how to pilot it in turbulent skies. The plane's motions and behaviors would seem alien to it, and appear to possess a life of its own. Consciousness for early humanity exhibited this exact behavior. As an evolving species on this planet, we began to utilize the billions of neurological connections that compose this vast array of nerves and cells called the brain. The additive component of this change involved the blooming of new synapses in response to controlling a complex environment. By forming a large variety and number of new connections, the brain can select the combinations that work best. In doing so, the developing brain retains useful connections from its initial oversupply of synapses. The early stages of this evolutionary change would appear as a separate event or entity within us. This would correlate to the fact that the *cerebrum* is considered the seat of intelligence where higher processes of human thought exist. From this area of the brain comes speech, the ability to read, write and make calculations. Additionally, the higher aesthetic or creative side of the *cerebrum* is also the brain area for the composition of music, works of art and philosophical thought.

At this stage of evolution, this creative side of self would run hard against the grain of our earlier more primate nature. The early stages of insight, intuition and complex thought would appear to us as if another entity or ghost moved about our world. The reader can likely attest to having the experience of a sudden insight or revelation of thought when casually moving about their day. This feeling of an *Ah-ha* or insightful moment even now appears to come from outside of the self. The current theory towards understanding how or where this flash of insight originates is what we term our subconscious mind. Here the reader should note that modern humanity terms it "our" subconscious mind, alluding to the fact that it is in our possession and not an external organ. Early humanity, still transitioning to an evolved sense of self, may have experienced this suddenness of insight as solely an external event. Our ancestors would in no way appear or behave as humanity does today. We can aptly speculate that they moved about a world perceived through a completely different set of paradigms and realities. Our ancestors would appear alien to us, they would sound, look and act as if they were another species from another branch of the evolutionary tree. Similarly, we too will appear exactly as they did to our future distant relatives. How can we confirm what these forerunners of our generation felt and saw from their conscious perspective? Again and as quoted above by Owen Barfield, written language is our best hope in understanding the psychological evolution of consciousness. We have to examine the written word using current history as our guideline.

Condensing our Hominid Psychological-Evolutionary Timeline to recent history, we can map out the following over the last 10,000 years:

Hominid Psycholoigical Evolutionary Timeline

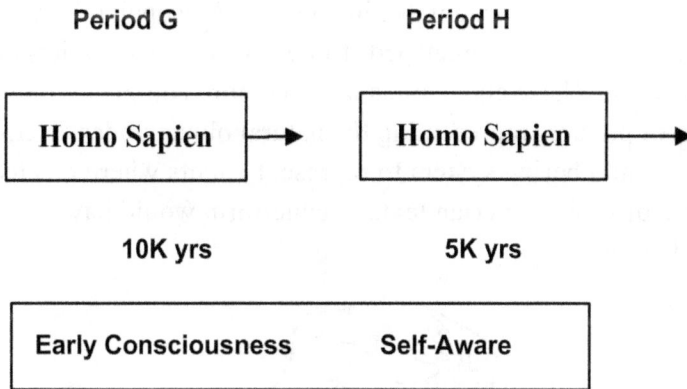

Period G	Period H

Homo Sapien $\rightarrow$	Homo Sapien $\rightarrow$

10K yrs	5K yrs

Early Consciousness	Self-Aware

Starting at the 10,000 Year mark or Period G, we see the written word take shape. As history records it, thousands of the languages spoken in the world today where founded and originated in Africa. Languages link to each other by common words, the theory being that members of each group have descended from a common language or ancestor. Original languages as defined by many scholars, originated just a few thousand years ago. This point is surprising in and of itself as it implies that consciousness as an evolutionary development is a recent phenomenon. The majority of languages have descended from the language of a tribe of nomads. As recently from 3000 BC to 2000 BC, humans spoke Indo-European languages that extended into Asia, the Iranian plateau and much of India. The Semitic languages originating from the language of tribal groups in Arabia around 3000 BC, is the spoken language over a large tract of territory from southern Arabia to the north of Syria.

From the Babylonians and Assyrians to the Hebrews and Phoenicians, Aramaic becomes the more common language of the Middle East. During this time, we see a flourishing of written texts, tablets, codices and recordings. During Period H of our above chart and over the last five thousand years, we gain a better understanding of the written texts studied by scholars today. What does this text tell us as it relates to the predominant mindset of our ancestors? If we look at early Sumerian writings, humans who lived on the banks of the Tigris and the Euphrates in southern Mesopotamia, we see a writing system of wedge-shaped strokes in small clay tablets known as cuneiform. These clay tablets became more complex with the inclusion of pictures representing the natural object under discussion. Further, a numbering system to represent counts where created. An example of what Sumerian texts in cuneiform would have appeared like is below:

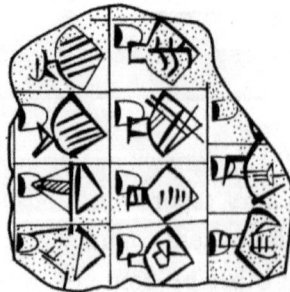

On Being the Being

Some of the earliest texts found in the Sumerian cities of Uruk and Jamdat Nasr around 3000 BCE, had a large number of monosyllabic words. We would hear in translation of a clay tablets similar to the picture above, "3 acres wheat for harvest / field of wool trees / seal luga-emahe". As we read this, the flow of words would likely sound very monotone and limited in expression. Around 2500 BCE, their writing systems started to exhibit phonetic elements and complex constructions from the original single word per symbol form. From these and other written texts, we gain insight into the level of consciousness of humanity as it relates to the environment and individual. As noted in William Calvin's description of individuals with frontal lobe dysfunction, we can speculate on humanity's psychological makeup during this time. What we see is less expressive texts as it relates to complex emotions. Again, this is not to imply that early humans were dysfunctional in any way but rather, they were our great forerunners evolving through a major psychological change. As a final note, the Sumerian language was the common language used through the 1st century CE, and was one of the longest used writing systems in history.

If we move forward through the time of the Mesopotamian peoples, those of the Babylonians, Assyrians, Persians and others, we see an adaptation of the Sumerian system of writing. This writing system was modified by these peoples so that it symbols became positional very much like our current style of writing. Similar to how our current Latin based language roots persist, the Sumerian form persisted for the Mesopotamians. To put our hands around the evolution of consciousness as it corresponds to that of languages, we can sketch out the following chart to aid us:

Hominid Psychological Evolutionary
Language Timeline

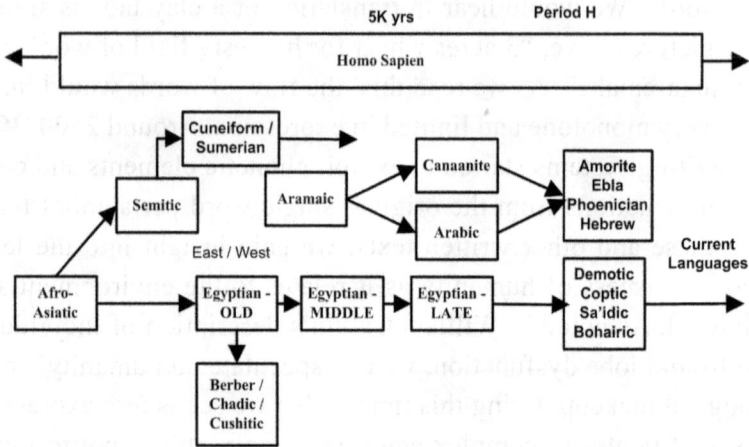

Please keep in mind, this chart is in no way inclusive of all languages spoken or written throughout this time. The Sumerian appears to have all but died out as a spoken language by the end of the III Dynasty of Ur, c.2000 BC. The Egyptian language died out as a spoken language as recently as the 17th century AD under the influence of the Arabic languages. Our closest and most familiar connection to the Aramaic language comes from the Christian and Jewish texts of the Bible originally written in a form of Aramaic. In order to begin our analysis of modern languages as it relates to the evolution of consciousness, let us turn our attention to the Old and New Testament of the Bible. In the old testament of the King James Version of the Bible, written between the timeframe of 300 to 600 BC, we read in the book of *Amos*:

> "And he said, "The LORD roars from Zion. And from Jerusalem he utters his voice And the shepherds' pasture grounds mourn, And the summit of Carmel dries up."[9]

---

9. Amos, *The Bible* – King James Version, Book of Amos, verse 2.

On Being the Being

Also from the book of *Micah* in its opening paragraph we read:

"The word of the Lord which came to Micah of
Moresheth in the days of Jotham, Ahaz, and Hezekiah,
kings of Judah, which he saw concerning Samaria and
Jerusalem."[10]

What do these words and writings offer as a clue into the mind-set of these writers? In both texts, we hear the reference to voices heard and the tone of language is that of command and authority. What we also read in the *Micah* passage, is that of a visual event, a "seeing" or unfolding taking place.

As previously discussed, we see the signs of what can be termed a quasi-consciousness or surreal mindscape. The authoritarian voices in these passages also reflect what we can call the Alpha Leader or god-king dictates. Throughout these passages, and I suggest the reader familiarize themselves with some of this writing, we hear the term 'Thou' repeatedly used, can we assume that another *being* is referenced? Reading other texts during this period such as the Hindu book called the *Mahabharata* or *The Great Tale of the Emperor Dynasty* written around 500 BC, the following is stated:

"Hear, O Sanjaya, all that happened thereupon and came
to my knowledge. And when thou hast heard all I say,
recollecting everything as it fell out, thou shall then know
me for one with a prophetic eye. When I heard that Arjuna,
having bent the bow, had pierced the curious mark and
brought it down to the ground, and bore away in triumph
the maiden Krishna, in the sight of the assembled princes,
then, O Sanjaya I had no hope of success."[11]

10. Micah, *The Bible* – King James Version, Book of Micah, verse 52-56.
11. *The Mahābhārata*, Adi Parva Section I, translated as "the great tale of the Bharata Dynasty" is one of the two major Sanskrit epics of ancient India, the other being the Rāmāyana. With more than 74,000 verses, plus long prose passages, or some 1.8 million words in total, it is one of the longest epic poems worldwide.

Here we encounter early Hindu creation mythology replete with references to gods and goddesses. The state of mind where knowledge comes to the writer is similar to the Biblical texts preceding it. Further, if we turn our attention to written texts from the Egyptian period produced around 1000 BC, we read:

> "[These are] the words which the god Neb-er-tcher spake after he had, come into being: "I am he who came into being in the form of the god Khepera, and I am the creator of that which came into being, that is to say, I am the creator of everything which came into being: now the things which I created, and which came forth out of my month after that I had come into being myself were exceedingly many."[12]

We encounter in the Egyptian words the implication of a voice that comes to its writer in an authoritarian manner. The mindset of the writer is a "seeing" consciousness revealing itself. This same mindscape of language and writing is in the Greek texts during this time. Below we read the writings of a Grecian priestess consulting with the gods for her tribe. These priestesses or Oracles entered into a trance-like state and heard voices that conveyed warnings, advice or pending disasters such as:

> "I count the sand, I measure out the sea, The silent and the dumb are heard by me E'en now the odors of my sense that rise, A tortoise boiling with lamb supplies While brass below and brass above it lies."[13]

12. E. A. Wallis Budge, *Legends of the Gods* (translated), (London: Kegan Paul, Trench and Trübner & Co. Ltd., 1912), pp. 2-3.
13. John A. Valko, *Conversation with Croseus Oracle at Delphi* (translated), The origin of the Delphic Oracle on Mt. Paranassus was affected as this mountain's sulfuric fumes had neural and physical effects on humans. The discovery of this was considered a miracle and a shrine was erected in the area near these gases.

On Being the Being

What we can note here is the rhythmic flow or singsong pattern of the texts that imply brain lateralization or right - side brain dominance. This brain lateralization seen throughout this period in numerous texts, further illustrates that early man functioned in a mind space very different from our present one. These texts show the same hallucinatory patterning we encounter in modern cases of left-brain dysfunction and early childhood. Please keep in mind that in our translation of these texts our references and modern belief systems inevitably present a bias. We must take the original writers of these texts literally, for doing otherwise belittles their meanings and our history. What can we glean from these writers and speakers as it relates to our conscious evolution? If we take another rough stab at redrawing or psychological evolutionary timeline as it relates language and conscious evolution, we might see the following:

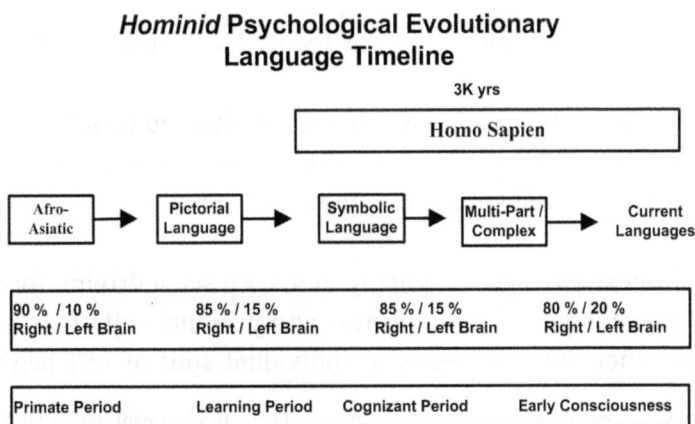

Hominid Psychological Evolutionary Language Timeline

3K yrs

Homo Sapien

| Afro-Asiatic | → | Pictorial Language | → | Symbolic Language | → | Multi-Part / Complex | → | Current Languages |

90 % / 10 % Right / Left Brain	85 % / 15 % Right / Left Brain	85 % / 15 % Right / Left Brain	80 % / 20 % Right / Left Brain

Primate Period	Learning Period	Cognizant Period	Early Consciousness

What begins to become clear is that this is what our sacred books and early writings have documented all along, our arduous and often chaotic rise to consciousness. As another example, we read in the Nag Hammadi, a set of thirteen leather-bound papyrus codices dating back to the 2nd century AD, the following:

"After I parted from the somatic darkness in me and the psychic chaos in mind and the feminine desire [. . .] in the darkness, I did not use it again."[14]

In the King James Version of the Bible, we see a clear distinction from the Old Testament (Older Witness) to the New Testament (Newer Witness) when we read:

"A pupil is not above his teacher, but everyone, after he has been fully trained, will be like his teacher."[15]

From the *Qur'an* we read:

"O you who believe! If an evil-doer comes to you with a report, look carefully into it lest you harm a people with ignorance, then be sorry for what you have done."[16]

As well as in Chapter 33 of the *Tao* by Lao-Tzu we read:

"Intelligent people know others. Enlightened people know themselves. You can conquer others with power, but it takes true strength to conquer yourself."[17]

In all these passages and many more, we see a driving force towards an awakening consciousness and personal self. This begins to occur after the many-gods or individual split of self begins to

14. John N. Sieber, *Zostrianos Codex* (translated), The Nag Hammadi dating back to the 2nd century AD, comprised 52 mostly Gnostic tractates (treatises), believed to be a library hidden by monks from the nearby monastery of St Pachomius.

15. Luke, *The Bible* – King James Version, Chapter-Verse 7 23. Swami Prabhavananda and Christopher Isherwood, *The Song of God Bhagavad-Gita* (translated), (New York: New American Library, 1972), p. 18.

16. Muhammad, *The Qur'ān*, The Qur'an is the central religious text of Islam. Muslims believe the Qur'an to be the book of divine guidance and direction for mankind and consider the text in its original Arabic to be the real word of Allah revealed to Muhammad by Gabriel over a period of 23 years. Surah XLIX 6.

17. Lao-Tzu, *The Tao*, The Tao also pronounced Dao is a Chinese character often translated as 'The way of nature'. In ancient China Tao is simply the way and order of the Universe. Chapter 33.

unify. This unification of self accelerates throughout history as the breakdown of the group dynamic occurs through wars and population displacements. What early humanity begins to create on an individual basis one could herald as the greatest evolutionary leap ever made, that of self-awareness. Humanity's internal conscious space begins to unfold. This process starts with the advent of many gods (many minds) towards a single god (single mind), then bootstraps itself into the necessary space of self-reflective behavior. What is this self-reflective behavior? If the reader could imagine a pink elephant or similar abstraction, an imagined space in the mind to envision and pictorially describe this pink elephant occurs. This mind-space, although taken for granted in modern thinking, was a hard-earned human development. What we intuitively do in a fraction of a second was something developed through millions of years of evolution. This mind-space commonly called imagination is the current process of internally out-picturing events. Imagination, in the early stages of humanity is likely that of voices and visual hallucinations. This morphology of gods and goddesses represented the early mind-space called the self. In order to illuminate this later stage of conscious evolution and guide the individual in his or her daily endeavors, a set of rules or governing laws were required. This is exactly what we see in the moral codes and dictates of every religious and philosophical system throughout time.

In conclusion, and taking a step back to the subject title of this chapter, let us summarize our findings. The awakening of self-conscious behavior was a huge leap forward in human ability. Although consciousness became aware of itself, at present this leap is only partially complete. We may be self-aware, but we have not yet discovered the true nature and potential of *being*. Throughout history, there have been individuals whose self-awareness had evolved more rapidly, which we currently call our seers, prophets and mystics. These individuals are examples of what we can characterize as small evolutionary leaps of consciousness outside of the norm of their time. These individuals were and are human beings just like us

with similar bodies and similar nervous systems. The major difference is that they have moved their consciousness away from a limited or artificial sense of identity. Similarly, there are also remnants
of an earlier stage of consciousness always present in the human
species. Humanity's great need to create a "special" *being* or god
"out there," is the desire for an earlier stage of instinct based awareness. In opening Pandora's Box of awareness, we left behind the
Garden of Eden. We have opened wide the gate to self-awareness
which excludes our earlier existence of self-directed instinct. As
we continue to expand our consciousness, our ability in the areas
of knowing, questioning, rationalizing and thinking also expands.
If we redraw and condense the above chart to capture humanity's
mental and emotional characteristic up to recent times, we may see
something like this:

Hominid Psychological Evolutionary
Characteristic Timeline

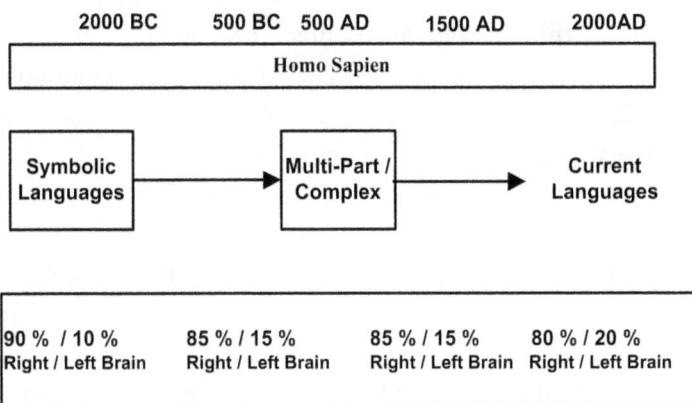

2000 BC	500 BC	500 AD	1500 AD	2000AD

Homo Sapien

Symbolic Languages	→	Multi-Part / Complex	→	Current Languages

90 % / 10 % Right / Left Brain	85 % / 15 % Right / Left Brain	85 % / 15 % Right / Left Brain	80 % / 20 % Right / Left Brain

Pyschological Makeup / Effects

- Auditory Hallucinations	- Loss Of Voices	- Internalization	- Mind / Self
- Tribal Mind	- Tribal Mindset	- Community Mind	- Global Mind
- Alpha Male	- Single God	- New Age Thought	- Loss of God
- Causal	- Causal	- Karmic	- Philosophical

Please keep in mind that we are drawing a rough sketch of evolutionary time and the psychological development of humanity based on translated languages. The point emphasized here is that we cannot take for granted the internal development of the human species if we wish to understand our past. If we had the privilege to step back in time and act as tourist during the period when humanity experienced its "Loss of Voices", we would be awed at the tremendous leap we made as a species. Living during this earlier period of internalizing voices and imaginations to the fuller recognition of self, would be nothing less than a staggering accomplishment.

All of this evolution was and still is the magnificence of what you are. We started this chapter in describing the living breathing tissues of the human body and its myriad of interconnected systems. Very much like the most advanced machine you could imagine, we saw that the body possessed a seemingly overwhelming complexity. Tens of billions of neurons, nerve cells, specialized organs, glands, veins, sensory cells and chemical messengers working together effortlessly. Our medical knowledge of just a few hundred years ago was limited to healing illnesses by excising the infected arms or legs with crude instruments. Surgeons of today use computer axial tomography scans (CAT scans), and magnetic resonance imaging (MRIs) tools, that reveal soft-tissue and other body structures previously unrevealed through conventional means. Even the invasive surgeries of today use lasers and diamond sharp knives to operate on individuals. In our continued identification of the synergies between physical body parts and mental functions, humanity is beginning to utilize holistic methods to understand the body's relationship to its parts as a whole. Current medicine is starting to focus on both the mental and energy influences on the body as opposed to just symptoms.

The continuation of this approach now recognized globally, will advance medicine for many years to come. These and many other advances in the area of medical science map very closely to our conclusions in this chapter. Humanity has placed its primary focus on the physical self at the cost of excluding its mental well-being. Scientifically, we see this through the extensive effort humanity has made in dating fossil record and the extraordinary discoveries in the field of medicine. Following in second place and likely occurring during the period of humanity's internalization of voices, is the exploration of the mind. Utilizing evolutionary data, written language and the arts, can we speculate where this psycho-evolutionary pattern will take us? Let us redraw our timeline one more time:

Hominid Psychological Evolutionary Characteristic Timeline

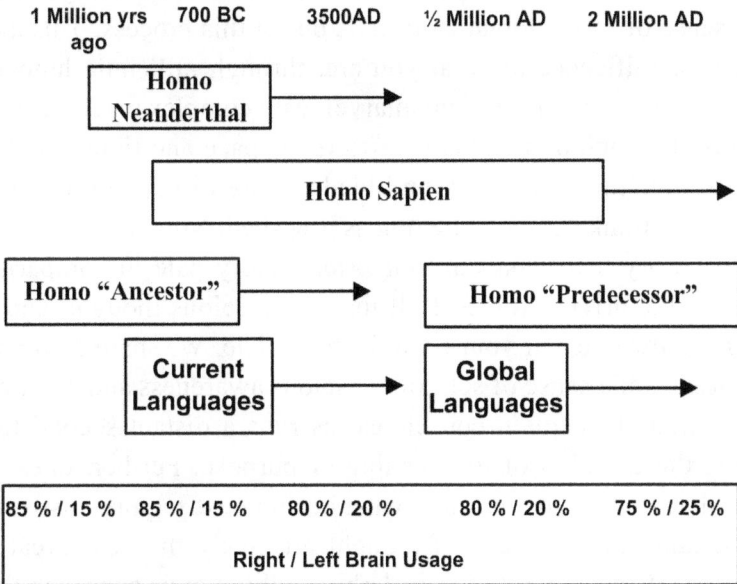

1 Million yrs ago	700 BC	3500AD	½ Million AD	2 Million AD

Homo Neanderthal →

Homo Sapien →

Homo "Ancestor" →	Homo "Predecessor"

Current Languages →	Global Languages →

85 % / 15 %	85 % / 15 %	80 % / 20 %	80 % / 20 %	75 % / 25 %

Right / Left Brain Usage

Pyschological Makeup / Effects

- Loss Of Voices	- Internalization / Mind	- Mind / Self	- One Mind
- Tribal Mindset	- Community Mindset	- Global Mindset	- One Self
- Single God	- Single God / New Age	- Loss Of God	- Self as God
- Causal	- Philosophical	- Metaphysical	- ??

What we see in this timeline are several things, on a physical basis the *cerebrum* or frontal lobe of man will continue to evolve. Based on this, we also see current and future members of our ancestral tree gain greater understanding and control of conscious thought. Also apparent in this timeline is the evolution of mind and self, what we see is that our global perception can transform into one interrelated mind and self. Looking back at chapter 2, one of our New Rules was that "there is only one of us". We can further expand on that point with the question of, when will we come to realize our individual sense of self is no longer necessary? A unified sense of self automatically falls out of this process. This again is the magnificence of what you are, through millennia humanity has fashioned a wondrous and marvelously complex machine called a body. Through unimaginable efforts in space and time, you have slowly sometimes painfully unfolded a sense of self, an individual capable of thinking and believing as it wished. Now we are crossing into territory that makes all our prior history pale in comparison. You are the driving force of all that is conscious thought, and the physical attributes of your brain is its vehicle. We share a common experience of a sense of self, of conscious awareness and emotional connection. To explain consciousness runs a distant second to us asking the question of its meaning or purpose. Further, questions like what am I, who am I, and what occurs next require answering. These and other avenues of thought are likely the next great adventures of science, religion and philosophy. Let us approach these questions by starting our next chapter with the question itself.

5

Why?

"Thinking gives off smoke to prove the existence of fire."
—Rumi

Why do we exist, what are we and why does it matter? In ending the last chapter with these difficult questions, we encounter an apparently insurmountable problem. Before the universe existed what was there, or was there simply nothing? Can we even approach these questions with any hope of comprehension or resolution? As beautifully articulated by the author Douglas Adams:

> "There is a theory which states that if ever anyone discovers exactly what the Universe is for and why it is here, it will instantly disappear and be replaced by something even more bizarre and inexplicable. There is another theory which states that this has already happened."[1]

Before we begin to address these very difficult questions, we need to find a starting point that requires no prior cause. Humanity's assumption concerning the origin of everything starts and concludes with, from nothing came something. Maybe that is all we can say at

---

1. Douglas Adams, *Fit the Seventh*, (First Broadcast on BBC Radio 4, 24 December 1978).

this point and end the conversation. We can also speculate that there simply cannot be a universe full of stars, galaxies and planets and all of us are simply seeing this incorrectly! Based on appearances though, the universe seems to exist and something or someone is asking these questions. In order to put our arms around this philosophical conundrum, we need to understand our basis or condition of reality. Everything for humanity exists in the framework of time and space. Regardless of whether they exist independently of one another, or unify with the present moment is still unproven. Time and space as the philosopher Kant saw it was that of a *priori* or given. A given that allows us to comprehend sense experience. In this respect, time and space as seen by Kant, is a non-physical substance or systematic framework used to structure our reality.

In order to understand the what, who and whys of this existence, it is necessary for us to take a brief tour of space and time. Let us look at what modern and past thinkers have said on the subject. Life's meaning or purpose as eloquently defined by the scholar Martin Buber, does not define itself tangibly outside of the individual. According to Martin, existence is not a recorded event with any certainty beyond itself. Aristotle, Aquinas and Kant thought that life's 'meaning' is a beatific vision of the highest good. The concept of a highest good adds purpose to happiness and morality, but falls short in approaching the significance or meaning of existence if there is any. If we believe in a god based account on the meaning of life, we see that one's existence fulfills a purpose god has assigned. The idea behind this is that god has a plan for the universe, and that one's life is meaningful to the degree that one helps bring about this plan. Objective naturalists believe that 'meaning' is something that is independent of the mind, and can possess correct or incorrect purposes. This implies that there are certain inherently worthwhile or final conditions that confer meaning for everyone. If we objectify meaning, we need to take an in-depth look at the physical world around us in order to ascertain it.

If we look at the current theory on the origin of the universe, scientists tell us that very small and compact energies existed prior to a large explosion we have called the Big Bang. How long ago was this or when did time begin? Recent estimates range between 12 and 15 billion years ago. Data supplied by the Hubble Space Telescope refines this estimate down to about 14 billion years ago. Given that these numbers are staggeringly large, what can they possibly tell us? In essence, science is saying that based on a long life expectancy of a human, about 100 years, time would have began approximately 140 Million generations ago. The math and science behind this as-tronomical number is a calculation of finding the oldest star clusters we can visibly see. Stars end their lives at a point they have used up the hydrogen that fuels their thermonuclear fusion. In essence, a star like our Sun is initially born in a cloud of dust and gas, and when it reaches adolescence, it is halfway through its life. Then very much like human beings who turn grey and wrinkle as old age sets in, its sign of old age is that of turning into a red giant. When we see a star in a cloud of dust and gas, we consider it a young star. When it turns into a red giant, we know that the star is approaching the end of its life. From a distance, we measure this by its light spectrum.

Taking the size of a star and variability into account, if there is a star many times as massive as our Sun, it cannot be very old as the larger a star is, the shorter its life. The age of our Sun is about 10 Billion years old, its birth occurring about 4 Billion years after the universe began. The oldest stars we observe are white dwarfs, and they are the coldest and faintest. Blue stars are high-wattage stars (younger), and red stars are low-wattage stars (older). Yellowish or white stars similar to our Sun are in their adolescence. This pattern applies to the majority of stars observed as shaded in the following:

Young Stars　　**Middle Aged Stars**　　**Older Stars**

Blue	White	Yellow	Red

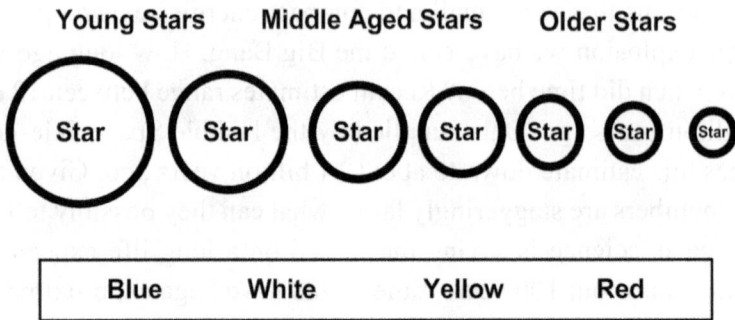

By searching for faint white dwarfs, scientists can estimate the length of time they have been cooling.

To measure the distance between objects we see in the night sky, astronomers have developed a number of different techniques. One simple method used is the shifting positions or parallax of stars over time. As an example of what parallax is, when you view an object in the rearview mirror of a car we see that it changes position over time. You can estimate its distance from you based on the amount of change observed. The greater the object changes position or shifts against a stable background, the closer it is to you and vice versa. If for example you hold a pencil in front of your eyes and close one eye while looking at it, then close that eye and open the other, you will notice the background objects change position. The closer you hold this pencil to your face and perform this test, the more you will notice that its positional shift is greater. Understanding this effect, in 1838 an astronomer by the name of F. W. Bessel found that certain stars were changing position every 10.3 years. The following diagram helps to illustrate this:

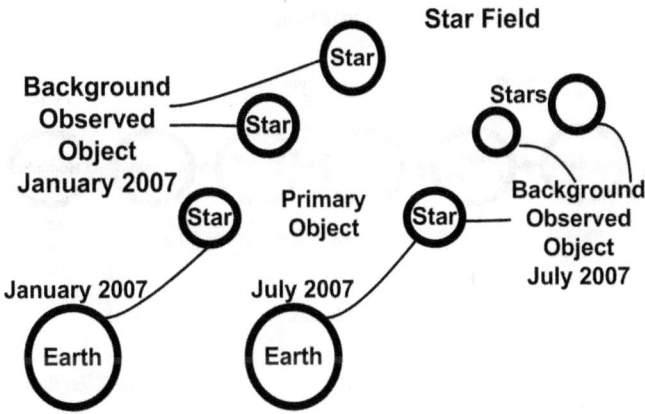

What we see in the above, is that the background of stars during January 2007 changed later in July 2007. Using this method, Bessel determined the positions and proper motions of stars, and created a mathematical model currently known as the Bessel function. This model helps us estimate that the beginning of physical creation occurred approximately 14 billion years ago. Again, scientists believe that somewhere in the vast void of space or time, the interactions of very compact quantities of enormous energy lead to an explosion we have called the Big Bang. If we attempt to draw a picture of our current understanding of creation, we would see something as pictured below. Please keep in mind that this diagram does not encompass all attributes of universal change across history:

Universe Timeline

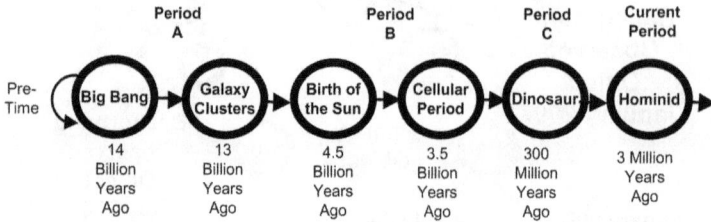

		Period A				Period B		Period C		Current Period
Pre-Time	Big Bang	Galaxy Clusters	Birth of the Sun	Cellular Period	Dinosaur	Hominid				
	14 Billion Years Ago	13 Billion Years Ago	4.5 Billion Years Ago	3.5 Billion Years Ago	300 Million Years Ago	3 Million Years Ago				

Main Events

Particles and antiparticles are created.	Galaxy formation	Proteins for cellular life.	Invertebrates and vertebrates leave the oceans	Apes walk on their back legs.
	The Milky Way forms.		Large reptiles (Dinosaurs) begin their ascent.	Brain evolution accelerates.

Moving forward from the time of the Big Bang, we see the initial clusters of galaxies forming in Period A) leading to the eventual birth of our sun and galaxy. The initial chemicals created during Period B) were the building blocks of life. These chemicals included Amino Acids, Proteins, Nucleic Acids and many others. Period C) denotes the early living ancestors of our planet up through the fossil record of mammals. Moving forward in time with a starting point such as the Big Bang helps us explain the shaping of the past, present and future, but it does not answer our premise of original intent or origin. The question asked was what caused the origin of the Big Bang? To assume a 'given' at this point only sidetracks us from trying to answer the larger question. Let us try to put our minds back around this very difficult question by looking at our diagram again.

Prior to Period A), we have called this region pre-time or the non-existence of time. The difficulty in describing a pre-time period is that we as humans have regarded time as an intrinsic given without question or cause. The assumption made in the above diagram is that an event or series of events had started some clock ticking. In the case of the universe, we have assumed this by placing these events in the flat plain of linear based time. The physicist Albert Einstein looked at the concept of time, and allowed us to view it from a new perspective called space-time. In a very simple and enlightening way, Einstein saw space and time as unified realities. He concluded that objects existing in three dimensions whose positions change do not solely exist in linear time. In essence, you cannot change your physical position without also changing your position in time. In a non-linear fashion, an object cannot move through space without the same force moving that object through time. Understanding this, one can state that there are no true stationary objects. By utilizing the speed of light measured at 186,000 Miles per Second, Einstein saw that the positional changes we measure are at a fraction of this speed. As an analogy to this, we could say it took you one billionth of a light mile to get up from where you are sitting and cross the room. In treating distance as the yardstick for time's measurement, we can now say it took you distance not time to cross the room. Further, if you were able to move at the speed of light we can now say it took you 250,000 miles to get to the moon and not 1.3 seconds.

Time as we currently understand it can be resolved into relative distances as it relates to the speed of light. Understanding that human beings move about the world at a fraction of the speed of light, what we have come to rely on is instinctual time as it relates to our environment. Based on this, we have created or invented a timeframe with much slower points of reference. Einstein helped us understand our slower rate of motion through his work and now famous equation $E = MC^2$. Translated, this equation states that Energy is equal to Mass multiplied by the speed of light times the speed of light. Beyond the radical conclusions we can draw from his work, a minor manipulation of the equation also yields C = Square root of (E / M). Measuring time relative to the speed of light as we have done, and using Einstein's equation predicts that light should move slower as the mass or gravitational force increases. This is due to the relationship of the energy of light to its frequency. A light beam traveling upwards in a gravitational field loses energy and its frequency goes down. To imagine the slowing of the speed of light, we have to envision a very large object, like a massive planet many times the size of earth, collocated with a beam of light. Gravity would slow or trap its movement.

To understand this from a practical basis, scientists used several very accurate clocks and mounted one on the top and the bottom of a water tower. They then noted that the clock nearer to the mass of the earth ran slower. Based on this conclusion, during Period A) of our chart all matter existed in a singular point, based on the incredible mass of the universe at this point, time was at a stand-still. When the Big Bang occurred, matter and gravity coalesced and different periods in Diagram 1) represent different timelines. For instance, the passing of a second 13 Billion years ago might have lasted 10,000 years as we measure time today. Taking this thought further, and using distance as a time concept, we can say that space-time as we understand it co-developed and represent the same thing. As the universe expands and mass decreases due to distance created by space, current gravitational forces began slowly decreasing. Based on this, can we say that time is speeding up? Modern Scientists agree that to describe the early universe during its inception is simply too difficult. Nevertheless, we can say that time whether measured or perceived is not a given and cannot exist in any definition of our pre-history.

If we look at current scientific views on causation or origin, we encounter modern quantum cosmologist views. The physicist Stephen Hawking envisioned the universe as a kind of self-contained entity. He saw it as an odd place where all possibilities exist in imaginary time. The theory of quantum gravity describes the early universe as a small and dense space of strange and unpredictable particles, where time and space simply cannot exist. Current string theory states that the primary source of matter is composed of tiny one-dimensional strings vibrating across a multitude of dimensions. String theorists believe that matter compressed to such unimaginable realities as in the early universe, was the cause of our cosmos exploding or colliding into being. A newer theory called M-Theory helps to explain the genesis of gravity and illuminates some of Einstein's space-time equations. The problem with these theories are that they never approach the origin of origin, or the bigger question of why did anything occur at all? There are many theories that push hard to understand the universe's past, but science struggles to explain original intent. The universe behaves as if it were working against our trying to understand what happened at or before its origin. What is missing here is that science by itself can only aid us in understanding the causal world, so we need to turn to other methods in our search. Here we read this same sentiment as expressed by philosopher Hegel:

"It would seem, then that causation is a principle capable of explaining particular facts but incapable of explaining the universe as a whole. But when we look a little deeper, we find that causation is not really capable of explaining even particular facts."[2]

Let us turn our investigation of original cause to what these philosophers have expressed.

What we know intuitively is that time *seems* to pass differently when we are young vs. old, happy vs. sad and so on. What we are really saying, is that time conforms to our current level of awareness or consciousness. What our scientific friends would like us to do at this point is to put this into a workable formula. Thinking along these lines, we would see an equation similar to this: Time is equal to consciousness divided by average life expectancy divided by the square root of energy (E). In a more formal shorthand we might write $T = C / Le * Square Root of E$. Unfortunately, we cannot use the scientific method at this point. In order to verify any formula or equation using this method is beyond our science at this time. The philosopher Martin Heidegger speculated that time measured from

---

2. Georg Wilhelm Friedrich Hegel, *The Philosophy of Hegel* translated by W. T. Stace, (New York: Dover Publications, 1955), p. 51

linear past to present was erroneous. He claimed that measured time was an inferior or in-authentic measurement. He further argued that to be able to define time ,properly, we needed to first find the *being* for whom such a definition would be meaningful. Implicitly, Heidegger's analysis of time relates to the conscious level of awareness the entity possesses. If we look at the average life expectancy of animals or plants on our planet, we can better understand his argument. For instance, if we take the average lifespan of a dog, on average 14-20 years, can we say their experience of time is similar to ours? We cannot. What we can say is that time is a kind of expanse of consciousness that is elastic from the past to the present. It appears that the now of the present moment is not an atomic now or a single pointed abstraction, but rather a slice of consciousness.

In our discussion on the concept of time, we first looked at measurable time from a scientific standpoint. The conclusions we have drawn were from a strictly scientific perspective, which we can now say are similar to what we are hearing from a philosophical perspective. The scientific view as described by Einstein, was that time and space are identical. Similarly, the philosophers Hegel and Heidegger refer to the concept of time as that of an intuited becoming. It appears that our existence based on the understanding from both these perspectives leaves us little ground to stand on. If time and space are subject to the perceiver, then our reality is subject to constant change by our perceived and accepted worldviews. If we adhere to this line of logic, we should experience constant shifts in reality wherever conscious thought is present. Based on this, we need to further our investigation on this subject. In a recent paper called *The Unreality of Time* by John McTaggart, he makes the case that time is unreal. From McTaggart's perspective, the distinctions of past, present and future events are essential for time perception. He argued that time is that of individual observation, and that a past event invokes change in the moment as it moves further towards the past. In his words:

"In the same way acts simultaneous with remembered
perceptions or anticipated perceptions are held to be past
or future, and this again is extended to events to which
none of the perceptions I now remember or anticipate are
simultaneous. But the origin of our belief in the whole
distinction lies in the distinction between perceptions and
anticipations or memories of perceptions."[3]

He proceeds to describe this in detail through utilizing an A, B
and C series that are different distinctions of perceived time. Immanuel Kant also argued that time is a form of inner sense which
structures and makes possible the cognition of objects. We see both
these viewpoints of perceived time also echoed by the philosopher
Heraclitus of Ephesus circa 535-575 BC. For Heraclitus, time was
an endless non-returning flow of change. He described it as a child
playing a game who maintains complete control of how the game
plays out. He described time as a transient concept under the control of its perceiver. We also see a similar description of time by the
Prophet Kahlil Gibran 1883-1931 AD. Gibran explained that time
is like a stream of water where one sits and watches, and that the
timeless in each of us is quite aware that prior memories and future
events are simply dreams we are privy to contemplate. In essence,
the original moment is always present and has not changed. The
eastern thinker Chuang Tzu 369-286 BC in his book *Knowledge
Travels North,* wrote that existence without limitation is space, and
continuity without a starting-point is time. What then of the objects in the physical world we perceive and live in? The Buddhist
teacher Dogen Zengji 1200-1253 AD, expressed that everything in
this world is intimately associated as time, and our *being* or the self
IS time. In his words:

"Even though you do not measure the hours of the day
as long or short, far or near, you still call it twelve

---

3. John McTaggart, *The Unreality of Time,* (Mind, 1908), pp. 457-474.

hours. Because the signs of time's coming and going
are obvious, people do not doubt it. Although they do
not doubt it, they do not understand it. Or when sentient
beings doubt what they do not understand, their doubt is
not firmly fixed. Because of that, their past doubts do not
necessarily coincide with the present doubt. Yet doubt
itself is nothing but time."[4]

The Taoist philosopher Wei Wu Wei 1885-1986 AD would likely agree with the Dogen Zengji and commented on this subject as follows:

"Time is seriality: Intemporality is simultaneity.
Therefore we may well be living at all points of our
'life', past and future as well as the suppositional
present, now and always. 'Now' is not a moment of
passing-time, 'Now' is immutable, eternal, and so also
forever in Time. Time, seen for what it is, undermines the
'self-nature' or 'reality' of every single thing on Earth."[5]

It seems that time, as defined by both our scientist and philosophers are similar. Time is dependent on its perceiver and subject towards its perception. Can we say that time as a construct of our reality is something created by us, and a pre-requisite for a physical world's appearance? Finally, how does this physical existence unfold itself to its perceiver as a reality? The philosopher Franklin Merrell-Wolff helps us with this when he comments that, "Reality is inversely proportional to appearance." Mr. Wolff felt that the reality we live in is in direct opposition to the degree of our perception. In other words, physical objects that exist for us as perceivers are the least substantial and ethereal objects possess the

---

4. Dogen Zenji, *Moon in a Dewdrop*, Translated by Dan Welch and Kazuaki Tanashi, (Internet: thezensite), Uji – 2.
5. Wei Wu Wei, *The Tenth Man*, (Hong Kong: Hong Kong University Press, 1971), Part IV. Time, Section 61.

greater reality. As described in his aphorism, "Though objects seem to exist, Consciousness-without-an-object is."

In Brian Greene's book *The Fabric of the Cosmos*, he comments on time as it relates to change and symmetry. For Mr. Greene, time relied on the absence of symmetry. Things in the universe must continually change in order for us to perceive a notion of conceptual time. In this sense, we may think of the laws of physics as equations involving a time variable, and say that these equations are symmetric. In physics, the "standard model" is a complex theory of quantum fields that describe the fundamental particles of matter we commonly know. What is controversial about these standard particles is that in quantum field theory, time reversal of these particles is one of several possible symmetries. This opens the door to non-forward moving time or present to past observations. As an example, we understand that if one drops a glass on a hard floor that it will shatter into pieces. What physics is saying is that there exists a distinct and valid possibility that the pieces from the glass dropped, can re-form back in the hand as the original glass or cup. This is similar to watching a movie where the cinematography is put in reverse, and everything that has happened in the past moment becomes the present. Although we can state with a high degree of certainty that this will unlikely happen, can we ask whether the absent symmetries Greene refers us to might not reappear?

In the Eastern Indian concept of time, we see that similar to other phenomena, time perceived is a static quantity rather than a dynamic one. This view does not affect their daily living where things of this world are always changing. What they believe is that the substance of the object is unchanging. Indian thought places a high value on universality, where the connection between the static conceptions of phenomena is not accidental as perceived. The Indian sage Sri Ramana Maharshi commented on the concept of time in one of his letters of enquiry as follows:

"What is time? It posits a state, one's   recognition of

David Sutherland

it, and also the changes which affect it. The interval
between two states is called time. A state cannot come
into being unless the mind calls it into existence. The
mind must be held by the self. If the mind is not made
use of, there is no concept of time. Time and space are
in the mind but one's true state lies beyond the mind.
The question of time does not arise at all to the one
established in one's true nature."[6]

Sri Ramana felt that time was an interval between events contingent on and or created by the mind. Similarly, Heidegger saw
time as the basis and the meaning of our *being*, and temporality
was the primordial structure of this *being*. Their analysis was that
of showing how the general structure of being-in-the-world of phenomenological time produced humanity's everyday experience. We
can conclude that this was a transcendental task, which is not broken down into moments but taken as a whole. We also see the same
scientific and philosophical concept of time expressed in Buddhist
thought. Buddhism breaks through the barriers of space and time
and sees them as unreal instruments used by the self. Conscious
states and their mental properties arise in direct connection with
states of the mind we call the past, present and future. As described
in the Buddhist scriptures of the *Digha Nikaya* also called the *Long
Discourses,* we read:

"Even so was my past existence at that time real, but
unreal the future and present existence and my future
existence will be at one time real but unreal the past
and present existence and my present existence is now
real, but unreal the past and future existence. All these
are merely popular designations and expressions, mere

6. Sri Ramana Maharshi, *Talks with Sri Ramana Maharshi*, (India: Tiruvannamalai published by V. S. Ramanan, 1955), p. 574.

conventional terms of speaking, mere popular notions."[7]

As described above, our everyday humanity as it relates to time in the Buddhist view is only the eternal moment or transcendental now.

So far we have taken an exhaustive analysis of time in trying to understand what this concept means as it relates to human existence. Our premise has been that time or change forms the construct of our reality and creates our perception. Perception is in-itself a key ingredient of perceived time. What we have learned from our scientific community including Hawking, Einstein and others, is that measured time is transitory based on the observer. Taking the scientific view of time to original cause, we find only mathematical uncertainties that point to a unified state. All of these theories utilize an event to explain further events. We can summarize the following from all these findings:

1. Measured time is a transitory measurement.
2. Time is a dependent perceived state based on the location of the perceiver and;
3. Time has no distinct or independent reality.

The issue we encounter with these conclusions is that our belief in our existence depends on the constant ebb and flow of pasts, presents, and futures events, yet is something that is temporal which cannot exist! Our goal in answering the many difficult questions at the beginning of this chapter required us to understand the basis for the question and questioner asking them. The framework required to understand our *being* is what we call the self, which has shown us that from a scientific perspective reality as a function of time is erroneous. We cannot base existence or *being* on something that does not exist.

---

7. *The Digha Nikaya* also called The Long Discourses is a Buddhist scripture, the first of the five nikayas or collections, in the Sutta Pitaka, which is one of the "three baskets" that compose the Pali Tipitaka of Theravada Buddhism. Translation by T. W. Rhys Davids.

David Sutherland

In furthering our inquiry into the philosophical world concerning time, we have read the words of Heidegger, Wolff, McTaggart, The Dogen Zenji, Sri Ramana, Hawking and others in our search for clarification. What we have discovered in summary from their writings were the following:

1. Measured time is a transcendent perception.
2. Time is a conscious projection of states of self, created by the self and;
3. Time is merely a perspective we call reality.

As we can, time is at best a temporal state conceived and created by its participants. The fact that time underpins the basis of what we term existence and correspondingly the self, shows us that the self is also a temporal entity. Let us take a deeper look at who this time-based *being* is as it relates to its temporal-reality, and its appearance on planet earth.

Consciousness as we have discussed appears as a consciousness of content. An object, thought or emotion, has to appear on the internal screen of the mind for consciousness to take place. In essence, you are not conscious unless you are aware of something or someone. Our current worldview is, *beings* are born then enter into this time-based existence replete with its pre-existing pasts, present and futures. The assumption we make is that the past prior to conception pre-existed as a reality for this new *being* entering-the-world. Correspondingly, we also assume that time based futures continue after its death. In believing this, we must conclude the past always existed for this new *being* with its myriad of conscious content. The problem we encounter with this perspective is that our earlier definition of consciousness, an existence of consciousness as content, runs counter to this argument. This new *being* through entering-the-world enters without the content of pasts, presents or futures. Content is non-existent to this *being*, as it possesses no perceived sense of self to designate as past, present or future. In a very real and contradictory sense, this pre-consciousness in order to become conscious, has to perceive all content as what it is *not*. It possesses no past or future so must create content as *itself* in what we term the present.

What we experience in our everyday time-based existence is not so much what we are, but rather everything *we-are-not*. The appear-

Being / Non-Being (Time)

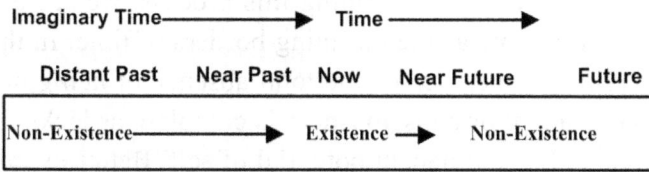

Imaginary Time⟶　Time ⟶

Distant Past　　Near Past　Now　Near Future　　Future

Non-Existence⟶　Existence ⟶　Non-Existence

ance of what *we-are-not* constitutes the bond of what we consciously perceive and witness. In essence, *we-are-not* that other person, place, thing or object. Based on this enigma, *being* which we will temporarily define as the present moment is a temporal state always defining the present moment as its existence. To understand this, let us draw a timeline of *being* and *non-being*:

What we see in the above diagram is that the distant past exists *only* in imaginary time. The self's appearance in what we can call Earth-time, is a revealed absence of *being* or non-appearance. The self does not exist in any context beyond its constant revelation of what it is not. If we look at the distant future, which this non-appearance of *being* must reveal, we find that *being* also falls into an imagined only time.

Only in this immediate *now* is there something that exists in the tension between what it is not. In the immediate *now,* the existing and non-existing is lost in the obscurity of the moment always past. All temporality or sense of self is concrete only for the individual believing in a substantiated self of pasts, presents and futures. In reality, its existence is contingent on the moment falling away from the present moment towards another present moment. This *wave collapse* of self or non-unitary change is by observation our *self* in pursuit of *being*. The potential of a self has been mistaken for the self. It is the constant pursuit of *being* that alludes to the promise of an incident of its meeting an origin. Yet, as we have discovered it is without origin as there is only the potential of its existence.

The self appears to be born into this world with a corresponding past alluding to a present and future. Yet, the corresponding past, present and future as created, are incident to its pursuit of self. If we turn again to our diagram outlining this process, we see a section called imaginary time as the outlining borders of time. In this state called imaginary time, we see the total absence of *being* or self in opposition. Content or consciousness is complete or lacks fullness, and predicts only a permanent potential of self. Better expressed in the words of the philosopher Jean-Paul Sartre:

> "The goal in short is to overtake that being which flees itself while being what it is in the mode of not-being."[8]

Moving through earth based time we take to this illusory pursuit of *being* through the self. The problem we encounter is our unwavering belief that a substantiated self or an existing *being* is our starting point. We pursue our own existence as if the pursuit strengthens the belief of a present existing self. This paradox can and has been discussed by the many philosophers, prophets and scientists, and often misunderstood by the public as contradictory language. Let us look at some of these contradictory thoughts summarized in the following chart:

---

8.   Paul Sartre, *Being and Nothingness*, (New York: Philosophical Library, 1956), p. 153.

On Being the Being

These and many other contradictory phrases relate to humanity's paradox of existence. We seek confirmation of a *self* by establishing a foundational existence as time. Causally, we approach this with *givens* as a bulwark against the process of unveiling the *self* for what it is. This *being*, you, cannot be co-present with itself in order to create itself. This would be similar to attempting as Alan Watts points out above, of trying to bite one's own teeth. If we look at this moment, we begin to see that its reprisals or context is the recovery of a *self* from the moment past. In an almost desperate game of hide and seek, we attempt existence through a succession of future possibilities in the hope of rejoining a *self* that is non-existent. This dilemma as further elaborated on Sartre:

> "But at the same time it is necessary that this being which recovers itself and establishes itself as a given— that is, which confers on itself the contingency of being in order to preserve it while founding it."[9]

The process of finding *self* or *being* is and has been the only dilemma in our understanding of *what* and *who* we are. We have

---

9. Jean-Paul Sartre, *Being and Nothingness*, (New York: Philosophical Library, 1956), p. 154.

learned from these philosophers and scientists that the individual as a conglomeration of events, memories and experiences, simply does not exist. *Self* is a quality thrown or released at the point of its attempt to create itself. Every instance of our reality is lost the moment it attempts at becoming. This is the reason we seek our *being* at the instance the last moment ends. Our endless pursuit to understand the whys of our existence is a contradiction in that our pursuit is misguided. The original contingency is our desire to justify or substantiate *self* as a *being* and its corresponding reality. We seek a reason or purpose for each moment and in it, an imaginary string of recalled moments. Time as a false mechanism of reality is a method only, a temporal means to a different end. The *whys* of our reality only exist as a causal call or revelation to this pursuit we call selfhood. As noted in our above diagrams of past, present and future realities, we exist as a transitory construct on the edge of a non-conscious state of *being*. We introduce this ambiguity of *self* for the cause of its very own existence, and simultaneously base the existence of *self* on this creation.

The logical mind cannot conceive that its own actions are cause and owner to its attempted creation of *being*. The need to define concrete relationships is the logical mind's original attempt to assuage, limit or transform itself to an inapprehensible god. We see throughout history man personifying god as self. The Hebrews used anthropomorphic representations of deity as in the phrase, *in man's image*. Similarly, Jehovah made man after his own image, and Jesus of the New Testament personified the restoration of *self* as god. In every instance, humanity is the phenomenal *being* in approximation to the primary consciousness of this super-being. Based on this, humans imitate self as the unrealized universal rule-maker that covets itself at a distance. This thought process simultaneously alleviates us of the responsibility of too much self-consciousness, and the ramifications of being in, of and for itself. The self or individual must indulge in a childlike game of character assassination by bringing forth itself, and then permitting the *self* to disappear.

On Being the Being

Our history is replete with individuals that have seen this game of hide-and-seek and exposed it for what it is. To insure this illusion continues, and the game and its players are reset we must eliminate those who expose the game for what it is, a game. Our definition and belief in a god must insure that it remains at a mystical distance to remain potent.

In bringing the concept of a god to our reality, we insure that the premise of its existence falls beyond the grasp of *being*. Hubris in the innate knowledge that we are this *being*, is implied in the biblical statement *no other gods before me*. Simply put, there is no other *being*, only the *self's* deception of *being* without premise or purpose is how the mind of humanity exists in nature. Why then do we maintain and nurture this ignorance of self? The philosopher Heinrich Zimmer felt that this ignorance or otherwise forgetfulness of our true nature was something we have accepted without just cause. As inexplicable as it might sound, the fact that we remain in this state is due to the concern that the phenomenal world we experience cannot exist as a viable reality. Western thought largely rooted in the philosophies of Platonism, Marxism and Freudianism, further promotes this ignorance through its dualistic views of humanity as inherently good, bad or neutral. Our coming of age in the modern world requires that we begin to understand humanity from a wider perspective.

What has now been uncovered and embraced in our philosophies, sciences and religions, is that the world takes the form of a transient reality that must eventually subside. In the world faiths, we see this in the transfiguration of far-east gods retaining both qualities of revealer and revealed. In the Hindu beliefs, this game exists as the god Siva engaged in the cosmic dance of healer and destroyer. In many Western cultures, this is similar to the contradiction of Son and Father being one yet distinct. In the scientific world, we experience this as wave-particle duality and quantum contradiction. These conundrums pose the greater paradigm of the initial question we raised concerning origin. Our veil of awareness called consciousness, must deposit *being* on the other side of a non-existent *self* in order to enact these dramas of creation and transience. We must fancy ourselves to be in possession of a divine *being,* while also remaining an outside spectator to this *being.*

To master this game of ego, we pretend our individual *self* is a complete reality and all about us are other similar complete realities. Yet to succeed at playing this game, we need to wear the mask of a *self* and a larger personality capable of dissolving itself at a moment's notice. The need to set an anchor in this game is what we have termed the inner light, Holy Ghost, Spiritual Guide, witness, observer or illuminator of all things. In doing this, we insure that consciousness is not truly lost to its delusion. In the Vedanta belief system, this delusion or veil of ignorance occurs in stages. The first is known as *sravanya,* that of intense study and learning. This stage of meditation called *manana* precedes *nididhyasanam,* that of intense focus. The final step is that of dissolution or the state of non-dualism. All distinction between the object and the perceiver becomes indiscernible.

These stages or processes of awareness occur for all individuals who have found the need to end this game of hide and seek. In the Christian belief, we see Christ described as a young man in earnest study of culture and traditions. In time he begins an inward journey towards *being,* which culminates in his departure from society for the forty days of meditation and intense focus. During his time away from civilization, he confronts the dualistic sense of *self* that ends with consciousness illuminating the game card. As described in the King James Bible, angels minister to him during this stage of awareness. We also see this same pattern enacted in the life of the Prophet Muhammad. During his youth, his learning period occurred through extensive travels with his uncle through Syria. Often he retired away from his group for meditation in the wilderness of the desert. During this time his confrontation with ego, similar to Christ's forty days in the wilderness, ended with the dissolution of dualistic thought. His illumination or the removal of humanity's veil of ignorance occurs as the angel Jibril ministers to him.

On Being the Being

Again we see Siddhārtha (Buddha) earnestly engaged as a young man educating himself about the world, before finding reprieve in solitude and meditation. Similar to Christ and Muhammad, he confronts the dualistic nature of *being*. During his solitude beneath the Bodhi-tree, he receives ministering from Brahma. Each of these individuals saw the transience of phenomenal reality or earth existence. As part of this awakening, the contradiction of *beings* existing in a world of sequential time revealed itself to all of them as an illusion. Scientifically, we saw that time was a relative existent co-dependent on perception and location. We saw that the scientist's ability to describe time as a *given* of reality was simply impossible. Philosophically, we hear Heidegger's question this in his book *Sein Und Zeit* (*Being and Time*), when he asks:

"Is there a way which leads from primordial time to the meaning of Being? Does time itself manifest itself as the horizon of Being?"[10]

What these thinkers, sages and scientists have discovered is that time and *being* are intrinsically interwoven with one another and presents itself as a conundrum. Both have no firm ground to stand on or can exist independently. As described in the Critique of Pure Reason by Kant, time belongs to the subjective-human experience and not that of reality.

The undeniable problem we discovered with believing in an authentic *self* is that it appears from all perspectives as something that cannot exist. The past and future belongs to a transitory *self* that exists within the psyche of humanity as something real. How can something that does not exist question its own existence? This is the last question we need to ask in our investigation of *self*. We have come to the understanding of the transitory needs of this phenomenal reality called consciousness, and the many dualisms we live by. In essence, we have gone through this process solely using

10. Martin Heidegger, *Being and Time*, (San Francisco, Harper Collins, 1962), p. 488.

a two-sided coin of logic, that of real vs. unreal, left vs. right etc . . . But as described by Heinrich Zimmer:

"One can describe it by neither of the two contradictory terms 'existence' or 'non-existence'."[11]

We can say the phenomenal mind of this *being*, you, is an approximate reflection of something in pursuit of *being*. Is it possible there is another reality, non-reality, existence or state we can describe or approach? In our next chapter, we will remove all obstacles to fully understanding *what* of *who* we are.

---

11 Heinrich Zimmer, *Philosophies of India*, (New York: Meridian, 1956), p. 421.

6

The Non-Existent Self

"Life has no meaning the moment you lose the illusion of being eternal."
—Jean-Paul Sartre

You, this chaotic myriad of emotional attachments, relationships, careers, values, opinions, objects and beliefs, define this "I" we call the self. The self, primarily composed of needs, desires and fears, believes that it exists and owns its identity. In essence, we can say that this person or that individual is a mass of interpreted value judgments based on culture, circumstance and belief. From these beliefs, we create our identity across the expanse of past, present and future time. Nevertheless, we know that this self, housed in its human body will eventually become non-existent at death. It is this absence of self, numbered in days, weeks or years that haunt us and defines its temporality. Beyond the self's desire to prolong, facilitate, plead or make concessions to survive, every moment of life surpasses it towards its impermanence. Knowingly we approach a sudden and probably ineffable phenomenon the moment the physical world ends for each of us. Death will be the transcendence of self, and its realization that life was a temporal reference expressed as a belief.

Our difficulty with coming to terms with this temporal expression of self, is due to perceiving a unified whole of self. This unified self of innumerable parts comprise its expression as a singularity that we believe maintains it cohesion. Yet, throughout our day-to-day experiences, we encounter numerous appearances that possess their existence based on their polar opposites. This we described as two numbers or concepts that reach their relative position of value, but become void when paired or combined. This is also the agreement between the many parts of the self to constitute and support the appearance of a whole existent. To begin to comprehend this massive assimilation of individuality, we must take a brief look at the genetic journey we have taken.

It is well understood and confirmed in many scientific studies that there is one ancestor for all life existing on this planet. About 3-4 billion years ago, a single cell algae or primitive life form began all genetic variations we see today. How was this determined? Geneticists have found the same genetic code mapped out to excruciating detail in all species of plant, animal and insect. Everything alive possesses the same genetic markers whose similarity extends well beyond a randomness of error. The implications of this are:

All existing life forms are merely variations in the code.
All life forms can or do possess the entire code.
All of life is intimately related.
All existing species are codependent.

In essence, your appearance as a self and body on this planet, is that of a very small island of variation in a vast sea of genetics. This island of identity or self is similar to a tiny upsurge in a much vaster pool of temporal appearances. Overall, your genome possesses an infinite set of possible selves. Self or identity as the upsurge or wave on this ocean of genetics is as much its trough as it is its crest. In this sense, your appearance as it is occurring is its own negation. Human reality or identity derives its meaning through its potential absence. To state this in a scientific way, our experience of identity is the wave collapse or event horizon of its *being*. In the clearest sense, you have been experiencing life as the missing entity.

On Being the Being

The difficulty we have in grasping this impermanence or lack of the self's totality, is due to the judgments of a reflective consciousness. The self's possession of a reflective consciousness drives this need. The constant desire to find meaning is the identity's error in assuming itself as the *being* (its essence) and not its appearance. It is as if a lion in its cage has mistaken itself for the bars of the cage. Can we ask, what is the impetus of this instinct for the self's survival, or what constitutes this nature of desired selfhood? Here we can only leave the questions with further questions. Is it just a mode of *being* or the nature of possibility misunderstood? From the obviously obscure position of self, we can only speculate on the motivations of *being* if any. Truly, we are standing on top of a coin trying to determine whether it reads heads or tails and worse, assuming that the object is a coin in the first place. What we can determine is that as a reflective identity, the temporal bond we have made with the self apprehends its own absence. If we take this line of thought further, we begin to see what the past, present and future might represent. They are the stakes in the ground of a self that seeks permanence or an eternity of actionable states of *being*. Is there an actionable state of existence, or an eternal repose that can fulfill the self's desire for continuity? Here we must take a chance and speculate on the mode of *being* from the perspective of self. Let us intelligently guess at whether there exists a coin beneath our feet and whether it is reading heads or tails.

Change belongs naturally to the self as the entity in constant flux of its appearance in the world. Martin Heidegger saw change or time as the making recognizable the temporality of our existence. In essence, when we make known or interpret change, time becomes present-time and can be understood as the 'now'. This applies to a past best described as a data point of references. Based on this, our understanding of a future-self is the awaiting of further data points from the 'now' which can be interpreted as a projected self. This is the foreseeing of tomorrow's events: the waking, eating, working, as well as, the self as its active participant. Time or projected time becomes the critical factor for the individual to justify its sub-stantiality in the world. But as we have seen, the self is only using the concept of time to recognize data points of 'now', 'then' and projected 'now's' towards its *being*. This misguided attempt to sub-stantiate self as its *being* is forfeit by the same mechanism. Our abil-ity of interpreting this referential temporality, time, does not make permanent the temporal. This is the attempt of the individual self to believe or make-believe, that there is always more time left or time available. The game the identity plays is that of using the temporal to create the temporal. In doing so, the individual can literally be seen as attempting to 'buy time'.

All of this leads the self to imagine an infinite time. The con-cept of an endless time is the self's attempt to make its way out of a temporal time or sustain an illusionary reality. Yet again, the 'now' divided into one or many reference points: the 'then' and pro-jected 'now' only masks the mortality of self. How then is this mask perpetrated or rather, how does the temporal self hide itself within itself? Here we raise the question of 'space' or background refer-ence. What is needed by the individual are additional references to add a more robust conception of the self's data points. In a pre-vious chapter, we discussed the innate ability of consciousness to create the necessary imagined event. This was the mind's internal space or landscape imagining an elephant in the room where none existed. Here the self is fully aware that there is no large mam-mal in the room, yet it is able to produce the image within its con-sciousness. Space then innately understood as the undifferentiated point or missing substance, is brilliantly attributed to by the self as a 'given'. As a minor segue, a 'given' or a 'because it is so' clearly shows the self's inability to surmise its reality. We need to ask the question again, how does self, hide within itself? We can say it does so in an ever deepening palimpsest of references whose endpoints take the form of a 'given'. Time is the palimpsest of never ending references guarded and maintained by the temporal self, and space is its endpoint conceived of as a 'given'.

On Being the Being

In our considerations of what the self is, and what it perceives as its reality, we can state the following:

Time is a referenced data point of 'now' and projected 'now'.

The self in time contains its reference of current self and projected selves.

All references or data points are codependent existents.

Undifferentiated space determined as a 'given' serves as an endpoint to these references.

We can conclude that the self's appearance in the world is an evolved reference based on space and time. In an almost game like way of smoke and mirrors, we imagine our 'self' as a parceled out time and space based event. Here it would serve us well to segue into a discussion on the origination of this appearance of self, but first we need to understand what these references represent. Our question is, how does the self create itself from these endpoints? We assume with unquestioning certainty that the little voice in our head, often called the little man or woman inside of us, is this 'us' belonging in reality. We give homage to the abstract notion that awareness hinges on this introspective dependence. This assumption being the holy grail of Descartes statement, *"cogito, ergo sum,"* 'I think, therefore I am', positions individual awareness as the endpoint of self. Nevertheless, we can only take our attributed awareness as a personal reference to self and nothing more. Descartes' statement brilliantly asked then answered, only opens up further questions into what is awareness and how do we define it. How do we ascribe awareness as a reference to self? Can we assume that when an individual talks of their awareness of someone or something that they are fully conscious when doing so?

As an analogy, one may be conscious of the fact that they are sitting, standing or moving about, but may not be introspectively aware of these things. This is similar to a drive home from work where you pass a number of objects; signs and buildings, yet in retrospect cannot say that you were aware of these many things. In this respect, you are conscious but not necessarily aware as in a focused state of mind. Can we state that the individual exists in the following states of awareness?

- Conscious but unaware,
- Aware and conscious

We clearly see that consciousness exhibits a passive but flawless means of maintaining the self's survival. Consciousness records in undifferentiated detail the content the self utilizes for further introspective analysis. We see this as the reflex in mental imagery that bridges the gap for self-directed awareness. Every individual waits for an unformed, boundary-less impression in consciousness to reach the surface of self for thought to occur. We are not aware of its processes or can describe its activity outside of the realm of reflective thought.

Can we begin to describe *being* as a state of awareness without content, where thinking and reasoning are things that we the self "do" as an expression of awareness? The fact that we have no introspective access beyond the vague description of an intuitive 'flash', might easily lead one to believe that something mysterious is at work behind the scenes. We can nevertheless approach this abstract thing called *being* from its absence as follows:

Being cannot be singularly aware or unaware.
(A directed or un-directed thought process)

Being remains a non-reference of or to the self.
(Present to self whether the individual is conscious or unconscious)

On Being the Being

Being is an unformed cognitive process or intention.
(It lacks origin or definition)

Although we run the risk of defining *being* as an undefined quantity, in doing so we expose the self in clearer detail. In his book *The Ape That Spoke*, John McCrone describes consciousness as a cascading series of neural memory and perception networks within the brain. These myriad of nerves and firing networks race across the cerebral cortex, and provide us a continuous sense of identity and waking awareness. He attributes our ability of recall to the invention of language. In his words:

> "Self-consciousness is clearly based on this artificial
> memory control that came with language. Self awareness
> is properly defined as the ability to see and remember
> what goes on in our own minds – the ability to think
> about our own thoughts, relive old experiences, and
> recapture old feelings."[1]

This continuous habit of recall and reflection creates a hazy reflexive pattern of behaviors we have come to identify as our individual selves. In our everyday life of working and dealing with other individuals, we re-animate this cloud of established behaviors and patterns. We experience this as the individual wakes from a night of sleep, and slowly, often clumsily starts their day in a hazy torpor of recollection. The brain jumpstarts its neural net of activity we call consciousness in order to re-establish our identity. When the threshold of this neural activity drops below a certain level of excitation, we again fall into an unconscious state and the self disappears until the threshold is re-excited. As human beings, we often discuss our ability to make conscious decisions as a separate matter from that of the physical infrastructure of the brain. In this respect, we de-

---

1. John McCrone, *The Ape That Spoke*, Language and the Evolution of the Human Mind, (New York: Avon Books, 1991), p. 121.

tach the mental *being* from that of the physical *being* and treat the two as distinct processes. In doing so, we confuse the meaning of consciousness and awareness in order to judge both. It is common for us to state that an individual when behaving improperly is not responsible for his or her actions based on this bifurcation of self.

When we establish a line between the physical machinery of self and what we can now term as the non-physical identification of self, we create a shadow self. The shadow self when representing the active contents of awareness must by its nature be a speculative observer. It must lag behind the intuitive self in thought and deed. The illusion of this divided reality is so strong and determinate that any counter argument to the self's justification is met with fear, suspicion or pain. In Daniel's C. Dennett's book *Breaking the Spell*, he describes this aptly when he states:

> "Without ever being frankly aware that a cherished ideal is endangered in some way, people may be strongly moved by a nameless dread, the sinking sense of loss of conviction, a threat intuited but not articulated that needs to be countered vigorously. This puts them in a state of mind that makes them particularly receptive to novel emphases that somehow seem right or fitting."[2]

This suggests that consciousness does not possess the requisite efficacy to bring the self from its temporal state to a desired permanence. As a conscious creature, human beings utilize this filtering mechanism to assume its existence. Similar to the saying, "There is nothing new under the sun, but there are lots of old things we don't know!" we create the self through an endless restructuring of thought and experience. The means and methods we have adopted in doing this is what we can call our unique projection of self or shadow consciousness. As difficult as it is to accept, this you as an

---

2. Daniel C. Dennett, *Breaking the Spell*, Religion as a natural Phenomenon, (New York: Penguin Books, 2006), p. 205.

individual self is no more than a bundle of neurons piecing together impressions, memories and intentions in a organized and often haphazard manner. The loss of the cherished ideal of a permanent self is our need and receptiveness for the supernatural. We can describe this as the appeal of the self for its *being* and its meaning in the world.

The self's desire to possess a permanent position or stance, is its survival mechanism for continued existence. If we feel wanted, needed or required, the justification for continued existence can be reconciled. The renowned psychiatrist Viktor Frankl endured years of abuse during the Nazi reign in a number of death camps. Based on his witnessing of humanity's unspeakable crimes against humanity, he obtained knowledge on what life's meaning can represent. Beyond the immediate fear of physical death, he noted that one of the most aggressive fears was what he termed the 'Existential Vacuum'. This vacuum or lack of content in one's life has been the primary cause behind modern depressions, neuroses and violent acts. In order to ameliorate this 'Existential Vacuum,' he noted that we have embraced a variety of mechanisms in order to cope. In dealing with meaning vs. meaninglessness, an immortal self became a common belief. Thousands of religions and practices established have been created too bridge this insurmountable vacuum. Additionally, escape mechanisms such as drugs, suicide and excessive materialism to eliminate this void or suppress it has and still occurs. Viktor Frankl saw the search for meaning as the primary motivation in our life. His therapy known as Logotherapy helps humanity deal with this frustration of meaninglessness through a method of taking responsibility for one's own purpose and fulfillment. In his Mr. Frankl's words:

"As each situation in life represents a challenge to man and presents a problem for him to solve, the question of the meaning of life may actually be reversed. Ultimately, man should not ask what the meaning of life is, but rather he must recognize that it is he who is asked. In a word, each man is questioned by life and he can only answer to life by answering for his own life, to life he can only respond by being responsible. Thus, logotherapy sees in responsibleness the very essence of human existence."[3]

Logotherapy as further described by Viktor Frankl, addresses meaning or purpose as a self directed and created process. Everything based on the transitory self or individual is a choice between possibilities. The self must make its choice to define which of these possibilities will create the meaning in its life towards its self-actualization. Logotherapy is an active and open process of living that does not require a pre-requisite or pre-existing structure for the individual to accept. Viktor Frankl's personal experience and the many others he met in the Nazi Death Camps, show us that when the self or identity is without the most basic survival needs, purpose is still necessary and created.

We begin to see one of the characteristics of the self as a thing that maintains or supports a definition of itself regardless of circumstance. When the individual asserts itself as the 'I' that is thinking or acting, it assumes the characteristic of a 'Thing' within the consciousness. As a 'Thing' within consciousness, the 'I' takes the upper hand or role as this you or me. This is exactly the role the self takes when it produces the 'I am' of awareness. The 'I am' of awareness becomes the highest and primary purpose of self. Further and as previously discussed, the individual's identity revealed in time contains its references of current self and projected self. Its temporality is its projection into an unknown horizon of future selves. Unique to the human animal is its innate ability to elaborate on the present, past and future sense of self. In a piecemeal manner, humanity unlike its extended animal family, has bundled up its physical survival with the self's survival. Biologically, we know that selfhood is not a requirement for continued physical existence.

3. Viktor E. Frankl, *Man's Search for Meaning*, (New York: Pocket Books, 1984), p. 131.

On Being the Being

The self as a 'Thing' within consciousness undertakes this dangerous voyage across the 'Existential Vacuum' to a shore beyond its grasp. This is the ineffable journey towards *being* within humanity's metaphysical belief systems. Beyond the definition of self, the answer to what this self protects is at risk at journey's end. From an ontological perspective, can we risk the statement that the meaning of *being* is a given hypothesis, or does this question asked by a 'Thing' unaware of its *being* even make sense? What we can say is that the self's existence depends on believing that within some alternate or temporal dimension, it becomes its own meaning. In essence, the self must believe in an 'elsewhere' for its survival. This is the first conclusion we can draw towards our understanding of what *being* is. It is the distant possibility that we exist as a presence intimately associated with the 'I' of the self.

We can begin our definition of *being* by stating that it is a perceived potential by the self, and assumes a perpetual existence for the self. We attempt to bridge the 'Existential Vacuum' with the belief that an immanence or divine thing must be at work behind the scenes. The self continues its qualitative definition of *being* by creating it as an external self 'at a distance' or in a possible future of selves. The problem we encounter in doing this is that the individual must also define itself based on this same mechanism of projection in thoughts and deeds. Our temporal self as 'Thing,' which suddenly exists and ends, is the struggle we encounter when trying to fix the self into a permanent phenomenon. Here we begin to understand that *being* exists as the moment, and is not something separate from it. The 'Existential Vacuum' is the bare unfettered moment of our existence, and cannot be historicized or made permanent in consciousness.

We see this expressed throughout a number of eastern schools of thought such as in Zen, The Tao (The Way) and Buddhism. Zen emphasizes the 'awakening' of the individual self from an egocentric pattern of awareness to a non-dualistic nature of living in the moment. It further explains that when we cast off our individual dualistic view of life, we begin to experience the 'here' and 'now' in its proper perspective. Similarly, The Tao emphasizes the naturalness of our innate spontaneity in each moment. This spontaneity is not that of a mindless or uncontrolled sense of self, but rather a trusting of our *being* as the moment unfolds. We see these same sentiments expressed in Confucian thought and in other schools of Buddhist writings. The difficulty in understanding *being* as our true existence is largely due to cultural mores that enlarge the individual as a self-owned reality. When we apprehend the individual self in this manner, we unwittingly lose the moment for a non-existent history of previous selves.

As an ego centered self, we encounter a false reality of making the temporal self a constituent to an imagined self or individual. The goal of the self is to derive its existence through a reflection of its absence or psychic temporality. The individual personality is similar to a mirror's reflection in a mirror that reflects a mirror. Our constant grasping to become a self by acquiring more experience, memories and personality traits, is the cause and effect of misunderstanding our being-in-the-moment. If we posit the self as a true reality, we would be mistaking the dreamer for the dream. The illusion of selfhood or its possession of reality as better described in the words of the philosopher Sartre are:

> "Here we are then in the presence of two temporalities:
> the original temporality of which we are the
> temporalization, and psychic temporality which
> simultaneously appears as incompatible with the mode
> of being our being and as an inter-subjective reality. . . .
> As for psychic temporality, it is incapable of constituting
> itself, for it is only a successive order of facts."[4]

In essence, the self is confused with the impression of a reflection of reference as a possibility towards its existence. The act of

---

4. Jean-Paul Sartre, *Being and Nothingness*, (New York: Philosophical Library, 1956), p. 159.

pretending or positing a belief does not make the act a reality or pave the way to a presence of substantiality. This zero sum game the individual plays in an effort towards obtaining their reality, becomes a psychological Gordian knot.

Where then do we find any semblance of what we are, and is the question even valid given what we now know of the self? If we pretend our existence resides in the shadow of this moment, a moment whose fleeting instance is lost on the next, how then do we proceed from here? We can begin by redefining existence away from the concepts of longevity, historicity and stable world references. Through a number of cultural mores and belief systems, humanity has determined that reality must have a relatively stable reference in order to exist. Further, memory should not serve as a cornerstone reference in order to insure present and future references. Finally, the assumption that reality must last beyond the moment towards an imagined eternity is no longer required. These beliefs are exactly what we grasp at as individual selves and create in our societies. Yet, as discussed in previous chapters, the world's stable references are at best in constant flux. In the area of historicity, we can only assume these events are facts based on second hand accounts, hazy memories and creative revisionism.

If we can put aside our entrenched beliefs in what reality is or is not based on our ingrained beliefs, we can begin to take a fresh look at this subject. What is perceptually directly in front of us may be unnoticed due to its proximity. Further, accepted cultural mores such as what is correct or desirable, sometimes stands in the way of seeing the obvious. As an analogy, there is this story of this Fisherman resting on the beach with his wife and kids. We encounter this family enjoying a quiet meal on this beach and a warm breeze coming off the sea. During their dinner, a young Businessman passing by notices the beautiful meal of fish they are sharing. He approaches the Fisherman and comments that his day's catch is quite bountiful, and would fetch a good price at market value. The Fisherman listens on with excitement and asks the young man how much more money he could make if he owned a little boat and could net more fish. The Businessman responds by telling him that with several boats, even better, with a small fleet of boats the Fisherman could make a large profit and start his own business. This further excites the Fisherman who asks the young man for more details on how to do this and what to expect in return. Again, the young Businessman describes how the Fisherman could expand into a large corporation with many boats and become a wealthy fishing magnate. The Fisherman now completely entranced with the Businessman's vision of this possible future, asks him to go on and tell him of his ultimate reward after all these years of hard work and effort. The Businessman tells him that he could then retire as a wealthy man, find a quiet beach where he and his family could relax and enjoy a quiet meal and a warm breeze coming off the sea.

As humans, we often have to go full circle to see what is already present to us. If we take a glance at what we sketched out earlier as our definition of *being,* we would read *being* is something that is not aware or unaware and that it possesses no-reference or origin of definition. What we begin to understand is that this nebulous or insubstantial definition of what we called *being,* is simply a description of the moment. Your reality in terms of events that may or may not require recollection is undefined. Reality cannot exist as a reference to a reference or in a reflected sense of self. The moment is not a nebulous or theoretical thing that will come about in some preordained future. You are this undivided moment, which has come then gone and will come again. From this perspective, we can see clearly the meaning in the words of Alan Watts:

> "There is only this now. It does not come from anywhere
> it is not going anywhere. It is not permanent, but it is
> not impermanent. Though moving, it is always still.
> When we try to catch it, it seems to run away, and yet it
> is always here and there is no escape from it. And when
> we turn round to find the self which is the moment, we

find that it has vanished like the past.[5]

The apparent contradictions in Alan Watt's words such as permanent but not permanent, moving but still are not contradictory, rather they are a clear description of this *being*, you. Confusion occurs for the individual mind based on its limitations and grasping to experience life as a causal event. The self unknowingly desires an either-or condition to hold on to and make sense of its existence. What we lose when we see life in this "on or off" manner, is the endless freedom that each moment offers us in experiencing life. You do not exist as a lifetime proposition with all the baggage of habits, history, likes and dislikes rather, you are this process of unfolding. Metaphorically speaking, you are not the fish in a large bowl of water called life you are the water!

This moment of *being* unlike the individual self requires no purpose or direction to exist. In this moment, all events from the microscopic to macrocosmic level occur without the slightest purpose or need for a purpose. In essence, the myriad of unseen events occurring on distant stars, planets, galaxies to the tiniest microbe compose this moment. Within this unfolding or being-in-the-moment, there exists an endless freedom or synchronicity. This moment humanity has described in many terms such as nirvana, bliss, Satori, heaven and others. We also hear echoes of these thoughts by many eastern and western philosophers when trying to describe this feeling although many of their words often come across as esoteric or ephemeral. As an example, we hear this from Zen Master Sokeian Sasaki when he states:

> "One day I wiped out all the notions from my mind, I
> gave up all desire. I discarded all the words with which I
> thought and stayed in quietude. . . . I lost the boundary
> of my physical body. I had skin, of course, but I felt I
> was standing in the center of the cosmos. . . .I saw people
> coming towards me, but all were the same man. All were

5. Alan W. Watts, *The Way Of Zen*, (New York: Vintage Books, 1957), p. 201.

myself! I had never known this world. I had believed that
I was created, but now I must change my opinion: I was
never created I was the cosmos no individual Mr. Sasaki
existed."[6]

Humanity's precarious relationship with itself and the natural world has placed its true being-in-the-moment, into a limited
cause and effect relationship. Identity as defined by humanity is
a carefully preserved pool of selected memories that obscure our
being-in-the-moment. These selected memories including conven-
tion, habit, purpose, belief and culture create a life of diminishing
returns. These diminishing returns create problems where age and
decay become inevitable enemies. Our illusion of time is similar
to the appearance of a moving background, when we know that it
is the moving vehicle creating this effect. If you look outside the
window of a car you are driving in, you assume a motion regardless
of the planet's rotation beneath you. Our difficulty in seeing this is
in changing our perspective from the abstract viewpoint, "the car's
passenger," to the concrete *being* (the planet). When we do change
our perspective, the world is no longer an obstacle working against
us. We experience the freedom that exists at all points of our reality.
Within the simplicity of being present as a part of reality, there exists no opposition for an isolated self. What we begin to understand
in the words of Zen Master Sasaki, is that an expansion of self occurs to the point of being indistinguishable from life. Is this perspective a licentious attitude towards living or some form of moral
abandonment? No, again we read in Sasaki's words all appearances
of identity, are not separate from the self, that "all were the same
man," all were this *being*.

We do not encounter a forced religion or spirituality in being-
in-the-moment, and we no longer feel displaced as a separate self.
Based on current cultural reality, we live solely in a past or future

6. Zen Notes, *the Transcendental World*, (New York: First Zen Institute of America, 1954), volume 1, Number 5.

while standing on the precipice of the moment. A moment that appears as fleeting phenomena that divides our reality into confusing linear events. The feeling that we are "chasing time" is the outcome of this single-minded view. A consciousness that attempts to understand the world in this manner can only obtain a fleeting glimpse of reality. When we release all assumptions and desires to create what is real and what is not, we awaken to the moment and begin the process of *being* in the now. This is not a superficial feeling or one that warrants amoral or inappropriate acts. Rather, the real being-in-the-moment begins to understand that it is aware of itself and need not interpret reality in a piecemeal fashion. This awakening is also not a realization of many moments within a string of events it is the realization of the endless moment of unhurried knowing. For example, as children we are not educated on how to breathe, eat or use our natural tactile abilities. These were all natural skills you acquired without trying. If you attempt to force any of these natural abilities using conscious thought, you would find yourself struggling to do so. Being-in-the-moment is similar to these natural abilities, it is inherent in the *being* and you are its moment.

Again, this is not a separation from a reality interpreted by its parts. This is a fullness of existence possessing no borders or limitations. This moment, you, requires no definition and is as omnipotent as it is impotent. Further, there is no danger in *being* or in not *being*. In the next section of this book, we must ask ourselves how does one live in this present moment, or reach this awareness of being-in-the-moment. In retrospect, we may find this question redundant, for like breathing, it is what you are and you can be nothing else.

7

My God, You are God

Deus factus sum
(I have become God)
—Erwin Schrodinger

Yes, you are god. Albeit an incompetent, naive, cruel and sloppy god . . . Nevertheless, you are god.

   This is a difficult chapter for it requires us to relinquish intellectualism, logic, spiritualism and established mores in order to understand this *being* in-pursuit-of-being, you. We need to throw our psyches up against an immovable surface and face a contradiction that we may not resolve. The means to do this requires a mechanism to bring us to the instance of realization of what we call the self. In religious and spiritual practices, methods for altering perception where employed to accomplish this. By using meditation and discipleship, we often come across the master - pupil relationship. In Zen Buddhism, a student utilizing deep contemplation called *zazen* received a contradictory puzzle called a *koan*. As evidenced in our last chapter's review of scientific and philosophical thought, our logical contradictions express the conflict of the mind's grasp on reality. We see that the many prophets, wise men and women throughout history have often used contradictory statements to approach a complex realization unavailable to the conscious mind. We hear Jesus of Nazareth making these contradictory statements with parables such as, 'the first would be last, and the last first' and, 'anyone who wants to save his life will lose it, but anyone who loses his life for my sake will find it.'. Some of these thoughts expressed in Zen Buddhism are, 'what is the sound of one hand clapping?' or in the 37th verse of the *Tao* by Lao Tzu we read, "The Tao does nothing / but leaves nothing undone.". In the same vein, we can utilize the koan to eliminate our conscious mind's logical grasping in order to begin to understand what the title of this chapter means. Before we begin, let us take a brief look at the argument or ontological conclusions humanity has made concerning the existence of a god.

St. Anselm of Canterbury believed in the existence of a god based on the conclusion that no greater *being* is conceivable. René Descartes also argued a similar point of a perfect *being* using assumptions and reasoning. His argument was that because we conceive of a perfect *being*, we must conclude that a perfect *being* exists. Immanuel Kant claimed that ontological arguments are unreliable based on the assumption that our existence is a requirement. Others also argued for or against the proof of the existence of a god relying on the arguments of it not being possible, or it being a possibility based on faith. In religious experience, god has a meaning only *if* the self or *I* exist. By definition, there are many arguments for or against the existence of a god, but they all resort to a logical premise of givens. This is the problem with our left-brain reasoning which painfully attempts to concretize life based on information only. In doing so, the mind is metaphorically attempting to squeeze an elephant into a teacup. The shift to non-dualistic thinking is difficult due to the loss of our cultural beliefs that define our reality from a sense-of-self. In non-dualistic thought, we encounter a mode of awareness that runs hard against the grain of accepted beliefs and social mores. We see this contradiction visually expressed by the well-known artist M C Escher in the following drawing.[1]

---

1. M.C. Escher's "Drawing Hands" © 2008 The M.C. Escher Company-Holland. All rights reserved.

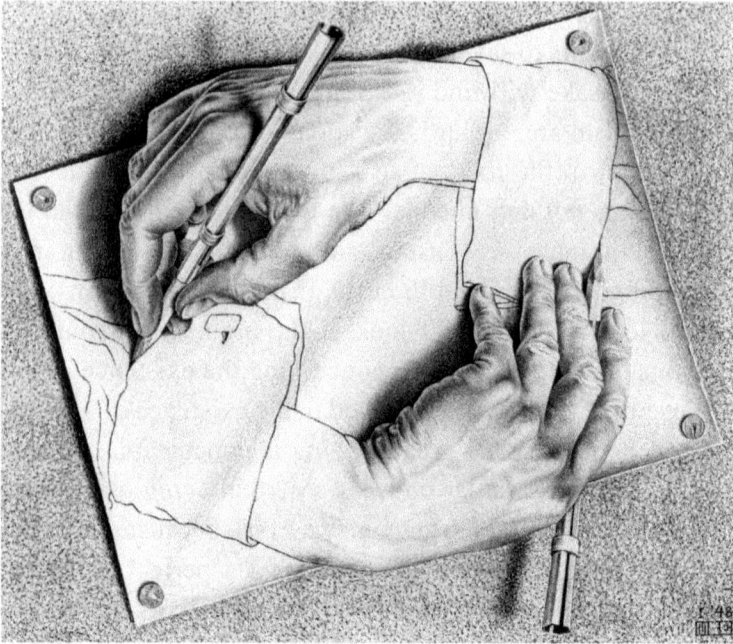

The mind's reaction in viewing this drawing is to dismiss it illogical reference based on the logical contradiction of a hand drawing a hand that draws a hand. We as humans quickly place this drawing in the category of a non-reality. Beyond the liberation of mind from conventional thinking, we might also try to use intuition in our observation of this picture. The concept used in this drawing is that of a vessel or state where something could be the origin of its own meaning and continue to create itself. To be both cause and effect or *Causa Sui*, is the conundrum misunderstood by the individual mind. Irrespective of this conundrum, current accepted religious views finds reason for an uncaused or non-contingent *being* and call it god. The problem with this uncaused *being* is that it never attempts to prove anything about its *prima facie* or sufficient evidence of itself.

Our discussion up to this point has shown that god or *being* is a relativistic statement contingent on the state of awareness of its perceiver. A perceiver created by the process as opposed to its reality.

On Being the Being

We can approach this contradiction by equating cause and effect, and assuming each is in possession of its opposite. In essence, we would be saying M. C. Escher's hand pre-possessed itself at some state towards its own creation. In this argument, reality is self-created. Yet, as appealing as the argument sounds, the thought of consciousness birthing consciousness provides us only further abstraction. The essence of self as its own cause presents us only with another given. As commented on by the philosopher Nietzsche, this creates only an inflated ego possessing itself. We cannot assume a given in our discussion in order to overcome a given. This takes us on a convoluted line of logic as the philosopher writes:

> "In order to be a project of founding itself, the in-itself would of necessity have to be originally a presence to itself—i.e., it would have to be already consciousness."[2]

In short, the in-itself referred to by Sartre represents the objects in the external world, a mode of existence that simply *IS* and unconscious. Further, the self as referenced above, manifests itself through the object and is never simply that object but the force that shaped it. The conclusion drawn from this is that it makes no sense in seeking a prior cause of *being* as it relates to the self. Its existence is bound to the force that shaped it. To ask and answer these difficult questions of created vs. self-created, we need to redefine our definition of creator based on all we have discovered so far.

When confronted with the difficult question of whether something can be self-created, we instinctively rely on our sensual world of cause and effect. This law simply states that for every effect there must be a cause. As an example, a glass or cup dropped could be an effect, and the cause of that effect is the hand releasing the glass or cup and the force of gravity accelerating it to the ground. In this fashion, humanity has compartmentalized life into causes and effects

---

2. Jean-Paul Sartre, *Being and Nothingness*, (New York: Philosophical Library, 1956), p. 621.

that follow this line of logic to the question of what caused the cause. This line of logic reflects the amount of effect relative to the size of the cause. As an example, we understand that it takes more energy (cause) to build a house (effect) than it would to close your hand and pick up a pencil. This implies that the universe is a relative effect based on a magnitude of causes. However, every bit of scientific evidence we have indicates that the universes' cause occurred at the most miniscule levels of a compact unified singularity.

Understanding this, we see only a replication of causes interpreted as variations of effects. The house under construction (cause) does not create a single effect. Instead, there are a number of coordinated events towards what finally appears to be a unified effect, a house. In an attempt to make sense of the largest unified effect called life, humanity assumes the belief of a massive cause called god. The problem we encounter when we make this assumption is that we perceive life as being that of a single unified event in a closed system. The contradiction is that life perceived by humanity is a multitude of varied effects that we believe exists as unified causes and effects. In restating this, we are saying that everything cannot or does not possess its own cause and effect. Larry Dossey in his book *Recovering the Soul*, argues that the development of all biological processes inherently possess their own unique pattern of organization. These characteristic patterns of organizations within the physical processes are also within our individual consciousnesses. On collective levels of social, political and cultural life, we encounter shared opinions, views, perceptions and reactions. This occurrence is seen when unrelated groups of individuals separated by large sections of time and space, construct similar structures such as the pyramids in Egypt and Mexico. Multiple independent discoveries in science including the simultaneous discovery of chromosomes in 1902, mathematical theorems, medicines and other discoveries show that events are inherent within the process.

In Buddhism, this is termed "Dependent Origination", which widens rather than limits the relationship that exists between cause and effect. In essence, causality does not occur based on this be-lief. The definition of cause and effect cannot precede or follow one or the other in any way. The problem we encounter in a linear world based on the concept of time and space, is that we build in the concept of delay or time passing. Without this temporal effect, there can be no conception of an independent *being* or external god. Throughout the Oriental Philosophies, we see this expressed in belief systems that do not pay homage to an all powerful god or central figure. Here we encounter the thought that the created creates, and all things exist as both descendant and ancestor. In Western Belief systems, the adherence to a strict linear model removes all objects and individuals from the active participation within life. This view restricts or filters out our being-in-the-moment, and the moment can then only exist in an imagined past or non-existent future.

What starts to unfold when we move away from a central god-figure, is that we can begin to see the creation and creator in every-thing. Our re-definition of god begins with the realization that we do not need to address a magnitude of unified causes for a unified effect. Within the smallest unit of biological life, we find unfathom-able energies that are fully self-contained and simultaneously de-pendent on everything surrounding it. Using Sheldrake's theories on Morphogenetic Fields as discussed in chapter 3, we begin to see the universe as a subject dependent reality. These fields of self-causation build up in a pattern of what Sheldrake termed *Causative Formation*. The historical view of a god of singular magnitude we can now redefine as a non-singular *being* constantly coming-into-being. The historical view of a god as a single governing power is the infinite multitude of life's patterns that guide one another in mutual evolution. From this perspective, we define god as the god called the atom or mayfly or woodchuck or star.

All of these particular patterns or objects remain equal in magni-tude, causality, power and mutual dependence. To define a singular creator imbuing all creation, not only narrows the act of creation to a linear world, it also defines a super *being* that by design is limited.

The question seldom asked is, what if you as were this omnipotent *being,* the all seeing all knowing creator? From the simplest perspective, this world for you would become a very hollow state of *being.* Consciousness would naturally encounter its own beginning and end. Nevertheless, let us imagine that we are omnipotent where everything you desire you create. Where would this leave us? After the initial high of self-contentment, we would find ourselves trapped in a nightmarish cartoon of unimaginable proportions. We would likely find ourselves as the character in the Rudyard Kipling poem *Gunga Din*, cherishing the blemishes, flaws and mistakes of a better person long gone. As elegantly expressed by Dr. Larry Dossey:

> "Omnipotence is pathological because it wrenches the
> wisher out of the natural order of things."[3]

What would a person's heart desire be after experiencing omnipotence where every moment of every day is the same? Would we be happier or insanely jealous over a time when we were active participants working through the vicissitudes of life, and what would we do? We would likely refrain from making little to any change to our individual selves or our current world situation. The anxiety to be right or argue against what is wrong would disappear. Fear of the unknown would be that of embracing all possibilities. Desire for eternal life, would be replaced with the awareness that we are not alive but *life* itself. From all perspectives, we would become unattached to the things of purposeful activity. This non-attachment as described in Vedanta texts is that of moving away from the constant urge of desires and the need to be right or wrong. In the act of simple perception, we would no longer take hold of the object, thought or emotion. We would begin to understand that perception is the first stage of the volitional process. When we release the personal needs behind the process of perception, we cease to be that which we never were. Additionally, the moment we enter into this

---

3. Larry Dossey, *Recovering the Soul*, (New York: Bantam Books, 1989), p. 194.

non-volitional state, the phenomenal universe can no longer exists as a causal event. As described by the Taoist philosopher Wei Wu Wei, we would then be 'sitting in a bodhimandala', a state of perfect availability. Our *being* would become the source of all dimensionality and phenomena.

Does this perspective of life leave the individual in some ineffectual state or ethereal fragment of a former self, or do we wander the cosmos without guide or protector? No, this new mindset removes from us the unwavering view that we are born, live out a disconnected life from each other, and then die with the fear or fantasy of an imagined heaven or hell. There is the god called the atom, the god called the mayfly, and this god called you. The issue we have in seeing this is due to our limited perspective in defining god. The terms omnipotent and omnipresent are humanity's aggressive vocabulary defined from a casual worldview of power. Our sense of omnipotence is literally that of having the power to bring about any state of affairs including impossible states or events. As we have seen, an imagined omnipotence can only lead to a grotesque state of reality. A reality where new possibilities do not exist, perfection then is a vacuous experience, and accomplishments are vain and hollow. If we philosophically try to understand what omnipotence means, we find only contradiction. Aquinas and Maimonides wrote that it is not possible for an omnipotent *being* to bring about an impossible occurrence, e.g. a square without corners. It would then be possible for an impossibility to occur which is its own contradiction. Better put, if an omnipotent *being* is powerless to do any one thing e.g. commit an evil act, then this *being* cannot be omnipotent. When modern humanity fully grasps its misguided definition of the severe contradictions omnipotence presents, religions world over would have to come to terms with its search for meaning.

Can we ask the question, what then can humanity do to bring meaning to its life, or what yardstick of purpose can one measure up to? We immediately find that these questions reflect that we are seeking an effect from a world-view of cause and effects. Both questions are self-defined givens based on our psychological self-created need for purpose. If we make the statement that life has no meaning, we open a Pandora box of questions and concerns. Reactively understood, this statement appears to be a negation of life and humanity assumes the uncomfortable condition of purposelessness. Humanity then has tied meaning and purpose so intimately together, that we assume the stance of perceiving our lives as meaningless. If we approach this statement from a non-biased position, it can be said that life in and of itself requires no meaning or purpose. In our drive for meaning, we see humanity's tragic failure to define itself with mental constructions of meanings or purpose. Only in the human species do we struggle with meaning and purpose. We see all of nature possessing its meaning in the simple act of *being*. As expressed in the words of author Samuel Butler, "All animals, except man, know that the principal business of life is to enjoy it."[4] How then do we feel fulfilled in our daily experiences if we do not attribute meaning to life? We hear the Dalai Lama express this concern when he writes:

"One great question underlies our experience, whether we think about it consciously or not: What is the purpose of life? I believe that the purpose of life is to be happy. From the moment of birth, every human being wants happiness and does not want to suffer. From the very core of our being we simply desire contentment."[5]

In reacting to what Samuel Butler and the Dalai Lama are saying, the egocentric persona instinctively searches for meaning within the causal world instead of within its own *being*. As simplistic or idealistic as it sounds, the real meaning or purpose of life is in the living

4. Samuel Butler, *The Way of all Flesh*, (Electronic: The Project Gutenberg eBook #2084, 2005), Chapter XIX.
5. Dalai Lama, *Voices from the Heart*, (Los Angeles: Tarcher, 1999), Compassion and Universal Responsibility, Part 1.

of it. For humanity to understand that it is more difficult to define meaning due to cultural teachings, we would have to invalidate these selfsame belief systems about the self and show them to be false. This circular reasoning creates the ego's emotion of fear, guilt and low self-esteem where we search for relief outside of the self.

The real problem rests in our misunderstanding the moment of our *being*. First, and as a definition of the term *being*, we can say it is this entity, you, posed as a question to itself in every moment. What does it mean to say that all purpose and meaning is sufficient in *being* or what is the temporal moment under *being*? The answer to both questions is that it is the authentic identity of the individual or thing. The conundrum we encounter is what Rene Descartes felt when confronted with the relation between the physical and non-physical worlds. He imagined a union between the two but so far, we have found no such abstraction. Heidegger saw humanity within the world, united with the world. Again, we found no reason to separate the *being* and its moment of being, the obvious relation to each other we found to be the same. As understood in the Buddhist text of Nagarjuna's *Analysis of Causality and of Nirvana*, we come to understand that our mental self is that of object. The contradiction this points out is that if we perceive ourselves as that of an object, we can never logically obtain the subjective counterpart of the self. In other words, our reality requires mutually cooperating conditions that connect the macroscopic and microscopic worlds within a network of events, purposes and connections. These events, purposes and connections form the patterns that enable our perception of a world.

Similarly, our *being* and its contents are inseparable and never predecessor or antecessor to one another. From a phenomenological perspective, if we look at this temporal state called *being,* we can only stand in awe at the human animal. This *being*, you, on a moment-to-moment basis creates, relates and perceives an overwhelming amount of data to a sense-of–self. A sense-of-self surrendered and recreated in the next moment. In Vedanta texts, this state or *being* is termed the *one-without-a-second.* We are this *one-without-a-second* in possession of no personal or divine mask. *Being,* which is a non-requisite state, is impersonal, anonymous and inactive. In modern belief systems, the unspoken goal and illusion of consciousness is that it acquires supreme virtue and becomes god. The many rites, customs and religious communities centering on a supreme creator represent the self's most subtle form of deceit. The question raised here, is how can a temporal *you* assume an existence beyond its transitory state? Let us now take an in depth look at this.

Within our analysis of what the term *being* means, we have discovered the following:

- Perpetual identity is a mask or façade used to create a sense of continuity.
- The moment of self is temporal, lost and recreated in the next moment. Reality beyond its content of consciousness does not exist.
- Self is the continuous relinquishment of self for *being* and;
- *Being* cannot represent existence or non-existence.

Based on the above, we now find ourselves caught in a closing circle of reasoning. We are now required to define human reality for what it is not. The philosopher Jean-Paul Sartre helps us with this when he writes:

> "The equal dignity of being, possessed by my being-for-others and by my being-for-myself permits a perpetually disintegrating synthesis and a perpetual game of escape from the for-itself. . . ."[6]

What is this escape are we undertaking, how can a *being* whose reality based on a perpetual game of escape from itself exist at all?

---

6. Jean-Paul Sartre, *Being and Nothingness,* (New York: Philosophical Library, 1956), p. 58.

At this impasse, the intellect begins its wayward struggle to grasp at meaning which is lost in the act of grasping it. Through the ages much thought and discussion along these lines of inquiry has mostly yielded more questions without answers. How then do we begin to untangle or understand this contradiction from a different perspective?

At the start of this chapter, we discussed the concept of what a koan or paradoxical epigram represented. Throughout human history, the many prophets, sages, wise men and women, have used this enigmatic way of discourse to suggest another perspective. Because the mind of humanity is entrenched in the causal or relative world of things, in order to break this bond a teacher-pupil relationship was established. Often a koan or paradox was utilized to help the pupil dislodge the intellect from its daily morass of distractions. The original term koan defines a document or statute of authority. The word later changed to mean an anecdote or question put forward to the student or pupil for the opening of the mind. A koan or a metaphor served to educate as well as, coerce the mind to realizations not available in formal education. Better described in the writings of D. T. Suzuki in his book *An Introduction to Zen Buddhism,* the koan forces the student into an inquisitive state of mind. This state of mind or attitude pushes the individual to a point where logic and the use reasoning has to be abandoned At that point, the student has no alternative but to utilize an intuitive or non-thinking aspect of their mind. This state is reflective of the enlightened or awakened state which many students and practitioners concentrate on during meditation.

Based on the many apparent contradictions a koan can present, the reader may ask, how can one paradox help in understanding another paradox? As an example, many readers are familiar with the term fighting fire with fire. Yet as contradictory as it sounds, it is common knowledge that firefighters use fire to control larger conflagrations. In this manner, our prior paradox of humanity's sense-of-being representing a temporality is approachable using a system of koans. Of the many koans, parables and metaphors written, Zen

Buddhism focused a lot of its attention on this form of information exchange. In traditional Buddhist cultures, the layperson or monk began with the precepts or standards on how the individual should deal with life on a day-to-day basis. When some of the more confusing attitudes and life styles had been resolved, it was then possible for the pupil to develop the mental stability needed to address these concepts. Throughout this learning process, self-realization or a greater clarity of the self became possible. About 400 years after Buddha's life, many of these insights were collected and condensed into precepts. We see the same use of precepts in all cultures including the Ten Commandments, Islamic morals codes, the Sermon on the Mount and others. If we look at some of the sixteen precepts from the Buddhist faith, we read the following in the Ten Grave Precepts:

> There is no killing.
> There is no stealing.
> There is no sexual misconduct.
> There is no lying.
> There is no trafficking in delusion.
> There is no slander.
> There is no slander for one's own benefit.
> There is no miserliness.
> There is no anger.
> There is no defilement of the Three Jewels.[7]

We clearly see similarities between these precepts and many other belief systems in bringing society and the individual to a state of mental stability. These rules of mental and physical conduct represent the need to bring the youth of mind into an awareness of *being*. From this more stable mental perspective, a solid understanding can be rooted in the living experience of daily life. Between what is

7. The Sixteen Bodhisattva Precepts are the basic teaching of Zen Buddhism of them *The Ten Precepts* (Pali: dasasila or samanerasikkha) are the precepts or training-rules for males and females, also referred to as novice monks or nuns.

wholesome and what is unhealthy, is the difference between what is open or closed. Without the stability of mental awareness, insight would remain beyond the limits of understanding. It is humanity's fascination with culture and ritual that has been a distraction to understanding *being-in-the-moment*. Here we see the same path that the prophets, sages, scholars as well as you are taking. Initially the search for self, then the self defined as object, and finally the meditative self exposed as its *being-in-the-moment*.

The riddle of *being* begins when we struggle with the emptiness that is implicit within the self. Revisiting one of our earlier conclusions that identity is a mask or façade to a past or present, we hear this further expressed in the words of the Chinese scholar Seng Chao (384 – 414):

"If the present passes on to the past, then there should be
the present in the past. If the past reaches to the present,
then there should be the past in the present. Since there
is no past in the present, we know that it does not come,
and since there is no present in the past, we know that it
does not go."[8]

In addition to the illusory state of a past or present, we have also concluded that the moment of self is a temporality created as a product thrown or escaping into the next moment. We clearly hear this reflected in the following statements by the scholars Zen Master Dogen Zengji, Martin Heidegger, and Lama Thubten Yeshe:

"Thus, the whole of existence, the whole Universe, is present at each moment of time. Have a quick look to see if you can find any part of the Universe that has escaped from this present moment."[9].

---

8   Hsuan-Tsang, *A Source Book in Chinese Philosophy*, (New Jersey: Princeton University Press, 1963), p. 349.

9.   Dogen Zengji, *Time-Present: A modern interpretation* translated by M. Eido Luetchford, (United Kingdom: Windbell Publications, 2003) Book 1 Chapter 11 – Uji.

In other words, we are in a dynamic present and not separate from the event or cause but included in both. *Being* is not passing or evolving in time, rather time is the *being* and its expression called the self is change. *Being,* is also described by Martin Heidegger when he writes:

> "The world is already presupposed in one's Being
> alongside the ready-to-hand concernfully and factually.
> . . . Thus the significance relationship which determines
> the structure of the world are not a network of forms
> which a worldless subject has laid over some kind of
> material.[10]

Similarly, this presupposed *being* alongside a ready-to-hand world, is the Dogen Zengji's description of the universe present at each moment. The paradox of simultaneity, the notion of events occurring at the same time at different places, takes us to our third discussion point. Reality beyond the content within consciousness cannot exist for the self. Human consciousness is limited to a prevailing content or sentiment. Based on this, the intuitive moment with its myriad of events is not experienced. Here we find reality beyond consciousness's current content as the universe present at every moment. Although it is available, it is unperceived by the self or individual. This is the self's constant relinquishment of self for *being,* or the individual's need to encounter reality in a piecemeal fashion.

These thoughts extend into territories we might not be comfortable entering. Our personality conditioned by culture, has the need to find meaning in the world around us. When doing so, we cast a judgmental eye on a limited set of events outside of our perceived reality. What are the events that occupy us? They are the natural disasters such as earthquakes, fires, tsunamis and others that can

---

10. Martin Heidegger, *Being and Time* translation by John Macquarrie and Edward Robinson, (San Francisco: Harper & Row, 1962), p. 417.

and do kill thousands of people. We perceive these major events and judge them as evil. In reality, these events as well as the myriad of daily events that affect our physical existence are impersonal. Reality is not biased or conditioned towards our individual masks or preferences. This does not assuage the need to take shelter, protect oneself or tend to daily living, but the pain we experience is intrinsically without bias. We can ask ourselves, how then does one plan, live or exist with such uncertain outcome? As a singular isolated self that believes its existence is a separate entity, we cannot. Yet, from the vantage point of the uninvolved witness, we can. This is the fundamental concept of the observer or witness, a *being* that is absent in order to be present. In the constant relinquishment of self to obtain self, we are unknowingly attempting to obtain this state of mind right now.

We see this equipoise or state of equilibrium expressed in all the great sages and thinkers throughout history. This is not a state of unemotional existence, it is one in which a wider or clearer perspective is obtained between the emotional event and its intuitive reaction. All of us have felt carried away by an emotion where our judgment is confused, and the reality of what we are experiencing becomes warped. As noted by L. Ron Hubbard the founder of *Dianetics*, the reactive mind of humanity represents the source of all our psychological problems. This reactive state of mind has managed to hide itself within the individual mind so intrinsically, that he felt it required a retraining of our basic instincts to overcome this and set it right. Hubbard saw that all physical effects such as heart ailments, asthma, high blood pressure and even the common cold were psychosomatic illnesses caused by the reactive mind. Relating to the world in a non-reactive state of mind, allows consciousness to experience larger emotional states of awareness without a false reaction. Detachment implies inner strength and the ability to function calmly under all circumstances. We see this example in the great sages and thinkers whose ability to experience enormous responsibilities left them emotionally unperturbed.

In our final point on the definition of *being*, we encounter the paradox of our causality. We can approach this contradiction by reading a koan found in *The Five Ranks* or *Wu Keng Chuan* by Tung-Shan Liang-Chieh entitled *Arriving within Together:*

> "Falling into neither existence nor nonexistence, who
> dares harmonize? People fully desire to exit the constant
> flux. But after bending and fitting, in the end still return
> to sit in the warmth of the coals."[11]

In taking a closer look at the above koan, what are these words telling us? Is there a conflict between our viewpoint of existence and non-existence, and what is the other state the author is referring too? Our initial reaction in reading this is to personify ourselves into the words, and imagine that the *constant flux* refers *to* our personal dreams, hopes and fears. We also read that after much struggling, *bending and fitting,* we remain with an emptiness of acts that echo in a universe of great discord. The word *fitting* evokes in us the sense of our basic reactivity, the many symbolizations and habitual patterning of our consciousness. The final lines, *in the end still return and sit / in the warmth / of the coals,* is the *individual* escaping back to the familiar patterning of the self. Yet, by default in taking refuge within this warmth, we create the circle outside of ourselves beyond the warmth of these coals. What are the two worlds we have created? In the words of the Lama Thubten Yeshe we read:

> "The two departments of ego and attachment work
> together in your mind, and as long as they do, whatever
> sense pleasure you enjoy, wherever you go, whatever
> friends you have, nothing lasts."[12]

---

11. Wu Keng Chuan translated by Tung-Shan Liang-Chieh, *Arriving Within Together - The Five Ranks*, A collection of 5 koans used in training in the *Rinzai* and *Sanbo Kyodan* lines *of Zen*. The koans deal with the progressive depth of enlightenment. (Cleary, 1995), p. 212.
12. Lama Thubten Yeshe, *Ego, Attachment and Liberation*, (Massachusetts: LYWA Publications, 1975), Chapter – 4, Your Mental Bureaucracy.

On Being the Being

The final line in the above koan, *who dare harmonize* strikes us as a question, but can it be an exhortation to peer beyond the circle of these habitual mental patterns? What and where is this path beyond existence and non-existence? We see this question asked and answered when we read the further words of the Wu Keng Chuan koan called *Coming From Within the Real:*

"Amidst nothingness there is a road far from the dust.
If you are simply able to avoid the ruling monarch's
personal name, then you will surpass the eloquence of
previous dynasties.[13]

It appears that the *nothingness* used in the above koan is a specific locale or destination. We see it described as a road, path or process that takes us beyond the familiar circle of warming coals described in the previous koan. Should we assume that this is a metaphor? Again, the concrete world revealed to us is a synthesis of totality in which our consciousness constitutes its content. Yet, as we have seen consciousness is an abstraction, and the very self we describe as you, me, he or she simply cannot exist. The koan's *nothingness* does not refer to an existing void instead, we see a specific phenomena whose inter-dependence is possibly unique. In contrast, our concrete reality is a composite reality composed of many parts of mutual dependencies. As a point of clarification, if we base the validity of a thing from an invalid basis, its meaning becomes obscure. The question asked here is, what did the man on the moon have for breakfast? In a similar sense, the koan alludes to the point that we are creating an illogical or invalid reality as a basis to describe reality. How does the above koan attempt to resolve this? We see in reading further, *if you are simply able to avoid the ruling*

---

13. Wu Keng Chuan translated by Tung-Shan Liang-Chieh, *Coming From Within the Real - The Five Ranks*, A collection of 5 koans used in training in the *Rinzai* and *Sanbo Kyodan lines of Zen*. The koans deal with the progressive depth of enlightenment. (Cleary, 1995), p. 212,

monarch's personal name / then you will surpass the eloquence / of previous dynasties, we can overcome our obsession of grasping for something. In summarizing our findings, we can now say:

— The Self is a dependent existence, and therefore does not exist qua Something.
— *Being* is a non-dependent reality qua Nothing.

The above statements do not imply an absolute existentialism or advocate a school of nihilistic thought rather, *being* is understood as a non-dependent state we can now define as reality. In essence, our physical world is this virtual presence revealed as consciousness. *Beings'* concreteness or our sense of reality is the asking then answering the question of what the man on the moon had for breakfast. In contrast, *being* shows that it is independent of our temporality, and simply requires no concrete definition.

In the Buddhist text *Heart of the Prajna-Paramita Sutra* commonly referred to as the Diamond Sutra, we read a concise description of the view of this physical world of ours:

"Form is emptiness, emptiness is form.
Emptiness is not other than form,
Form too is not other than emptiness."[14]

Form or matter is empty of intrinsic reality and exists as a phenomenal existence. The self is a combination of events that come together under suitable dependent conditions. Again, these conditions being dependent cannot possess a separate existence. Bringing together all of the above, can we state the following:

– *Being* is neither non-existent or existent and
– The individual self apart from *being* is an appearance.

14. Dalai Lama, *Essence of the Heart Sutra*, (Boston: Wisdom Publications, 2002), p. 111.

On Being the Being

Being as the foundation of itself serves as a mask to the individual self. Its opposite state can or does produce the temporal self. As an example, our physical reality describes opposite charges, which in the atomic world cancel each other out when brought together. Our mathematics also shows that the multiplication of two negative numbers produce a positive outcome. The negative number two multiplied by the negative number two e.g.: $(-2) * (-2)$, is equivalent to the positive number four $(+4)$. In a similar vein, *being* as an intrinsic state produces the illusion of a self from a non-existent reality. Self on the other hand is its nothingness reflected. As beautifully described by the Dalai Lama in his book, *Essence of the Heart Sutra:*

> "Cause and effect are only possible in a world that is dependently originated, and dependent origination is only possible in a world that is devoid of intrinsic existence, which is to say in a world that is empty. . . . Thus the world of form is a manifestation of emptiness."[15]

This individual self you call by name; Mike, Mary, Chin, Wilhelm, etc . . . simply does not exist. This non-existence experienced in every moment of each day, is *who-you-think-you-are* immediately being replaced with *who-you-are-becoming*. If we try to justify our existence as this temporality of selves by stating that time has passed between this me a moment ago to this me now, our argument falls short due to the insubstantiality of time. Time is the self in temporality, and the past and future moments are inaccessible states that simply do not exist. The mistake we have made is in believing that the self has sufficient reality to question its reality. What we begin to see is that *being* has posed the self as the question. Metaphorically speaking, it is as if a King (vis-à-vis *being*) from a very foreign land had sent its Scout (vis-à-vis *self*), to survey and assess its kingdom. The scout on its journey mistakes the task as its own

---

15. Ibid., p. 117.

and believes that it is a separate King or *being*. In doing so, this you, me, he and she, has lost track of the fact that we are the original authentic *being* confused as the self. Is this what we hear when we read the further words of the Wu Keng Chuan koan called *The Real within Phenomena:*

> "An old crone, having just awakened, comes upon an
> ancient mirror. That which is clearly reflected in front of her
> face is none other than her own likeness. Do not lose sight
> of your face again and go chasing after your shadow."[16]

What is the meaning of the ancient mirror reflecting one's own likeness? What we see reflected in this ancient mirror is the *being* and you are this *being*. In the last line of the above koan can we surmise what its author means as your shadow? Here we see the individual self is merely an illusion of light and form.

In our final analysis of who we are, we will not encounter choices relative to person, place or thing. The only question you have ever asked will need an answer. What is this question? It is the why of existence, the *prima facie* or cause of your own *being*. This paradox is even more difficult based on the understanding that this individual self never has or will exist. Here we encounter the ground of our and all *being*. The illusion of living in a casual world has kept this realization at a distance through distraction. The causal world we have created queries us with its ups vs. downs, hot vs. cold, good vs. bad and ultimately existence vs. non-existence. Yet, the *being* outside of these restrictive boxes has been you, me and everyone else. Can we ask what then was or is the purpose of this or anything we do? Yet taking this question at face value, we find ourselves creating these selfsame boxes of reality within the question. Simply put, true *being* is sufficient and can never desire to justify, validate or seek its permanence. It possesses no purposes or requirements for a purpose. This is what is behind the biblical conception of Alpha and

---

16. Chuan translated by Tung-Shan Liang-Chieh, *The Five Ranks*, (Cleary, 1995), p. 212.

On Being the Being

Omega; *being* is both beginning and end and you are this *being*. Is this what Christ meant when he stated in John 10:22, that he and the father are one, a single entity, not separate or distinct? In essence, everyone around us possesses the following qualities:

– We are born in question of selfhood.
– We exist with the innate knowledge of not existing at one point in the past and foreseeable future and;
– We strive to understand the unknown and create realities that can never last.

If we step back for a moment and try to understand what these qualities, characteristics, questions and conditions represent, it may strike you that only a god could enact or create these conditions. If we continue to see *being* as a singular omnipotent entity, our self-created state of duality will continue to hold the trump card over us. In Alan Watts' book *This Is It,* he reminds us of this when he writes:

> " . . .behind the urgent need realm of good and evil a vast region of oneself about where there need be no guilt or recrimination, where at last the self is indistinguishable from God."[17]

No guilt, recrimination and indistinguishable from god, is this not the state the self is seeking? Everyone and everything whether knowingly or not, must justifiably be its own creation and continue to create a newer self towards its *being*. As for the desire of omnipotence, as fanciful as it may sound it is actually a state of *being* and not an act. In an interview with Deepak Chopra he was asked about his beliefs concerning god and religion he commented, "I used to be an atheist until I realized that I was God."[18]. Yes, you,

17. Alan Watts, *This Is It,* (Toronto: Collier Books, 1967), p. 91.
18. Deepak Chopra, *Interview at Brightcove TV,* (August 5, 2006), *http://www.brightcove.tv/title.jsp?title=176904518.*

everyone and everything around you is god, and all we need to believe in is each other.

Our journey in this book began with us taking a closer look at our ingrained beliefs and the cultural underpinnings of our societies. We discovered that our general mode of day-to-day living fell into the categories of god, country and family. As summarized, our world-view aided us as individuals in dealing with the day-to-day events of our lives. Simultaneously though, we discovered that it also limited our understanding of who these strange and enigmatic beings we call *homo sapiens*. What we learned was that we created a split minded individual that required help in understanding itself. The balm applied to heal this split mind of humanity has come in the form of religion and numerous belief systems. Yet, this balm or bandage has become tattered through overuse. We found that this very private self or *I-ness* was what comprised our individual sense of reality. In trying to bridge the gulf between a false sense of self and the perceptual world, we have created complex and often inexplicable rules to live by. In looking at these rules, we took an in-depth view of what our beliefs were and whether we needed some new rules to aid us in our journey. In the second chapter of this book, we expanded our commitment to understand the self with these new guidelines and rules. Some of these rules were --there is only one of us and we are not alive but life itself. In chapter three, we began to look at the world from this new perspective where history helped us define this journey. What we found in our investigations were that early humans, utilizing their conscious mind, began to dissolve the boundaries between group instinct and reactive behaviors. Everywhere in the world the 'many gods of many tribes' began to unify into a larger singular god. This became apparent in our analysis of early writings and documents as we noted the distinct differences in tone, thought and structure of these texts.

From this perspective, we saw the formation of complex rule systems requiring group obedience and learned behaviors. As the mind of humanity began its harrowing journey to self-awareness, instinctual urges required mechanisms or rules to keep society intact. The birth of religion and indigenous belief systems aided man in controlling its evolving consciousness. In the next section of the book, we saw the rise of this *hominid* occurring approximately 5 million years ago and its magnificent journey through histories pages. Throughout this time, humanity recorded its thoughts experienced as voices and abstract reasoning. The fallout from all this questioning and reflection gave rise to the scientific world and larger religious movements. Questions asked by humans were, why do we exist, what is our purpose, and who or what is this strange, beautiful and enigmatic creature? Science showed us that the world model was full of contradictions. The concept of time and space was not explainable and matter appeared to be in constant flux. In turning to our sages, prophets and religious icons, we also found their answers wanting. It appears that both the scientific and religious communities found agreement in there confusion. The physical and unseen realms of *self* were temporal and a paradox to our understanding.

In an effort to understand what the temporal *self* was, we explored consciousness and content. What we discovered was that as an egocentric self our imagined reality derived its existence through its absence. The individual personality was similar to a mirror's reflection in a mirror. Through our constant grasping to become a tangible 'Thing', we came to misunderstand our *being-in-the-moment*. If we believed the self to be a substantive reality, we would be mistaking the dreamer for the dream. The difficulty in our understanding this was that we perceived self as a unified whole or individual. What we did learn is that the self's existence depends on it believing that some alternate or temporal dimension exists for it. In essence, the self must believe in an 'elsewhere' for its own survival. This was the first conclusion we had drawn towards our understanding of *being*.

In our continuing search, our last chapter brought us to a point of looking at a paradox through the lens of a paradox. In this chapter, we discussed the possibility of seeing beyond the confines of the relative world with its many dualisms. We surmised that the questions we were asking could be the wrong questions. To approach the concept of *being,* we read the words of some of our greatest thinkers and analyzed a number of paradoxes to help us unravel a paradox. Their many words and thoughts helped us see that the question 'why?' may be incorrect based on our current causal state of mind. In essence, this mindset only added to the confused dualities we experience. Only then could we see the possibility that within our clumsy attempts at self-hood, was our drive to reach our own *being.* This *being,* which resides in our social sense of what we call god, was our collective minds separate and conscious.

What we discovered is that you *are* this *being* and there is not, and never has been a separate mind. Whatever religious myths or rites we have consumed as humans have obscured this truth from us. Our desire for freedom dictates that this awareness is the self-created effort or project we have undertaken. God as concept, and as defined in numerous cultures, represents the ultimate freedom we desire. Many philosophers have surmised that humanity's only desire is to be god. The definition of this desire has varied, but ultimately an everlasting sense of *being* or reality has been the goal. Humanity of ages past has turned their eyes towards the skies with the belief of some divine balance. When we look at the matter from their point of view, we saw that the agrarian individual of husbandry and field required these gods as intermediaries. Within the modern world of global access and information, we find that our intermediaries are no longer required. It remains for us to determine our meaning and with it, our motivation for continued existence. Self-awareness or consciousness has reached the boiling point where we are now determined and designed through our actions, intents and desires. This progression of mind understands it possesses its own need for creation or annihilation in an abstract attempt towards defining itself.

God, you, can never be an all powerful, all-seeing, all-knowing self. The cardinal rule of cause and effect represents a dismal proposition for justifying a mode of existence based on omnipotence. *Being*

On Being the Being

or existence can resolve the difficulty of origin or purpose by us understanding that its reciprocal relationship or self, simply does not exist. This is the lathe of heaven or the path of hell we have chosen as we hold ourselves in awe of the passionate thinker, scribe, saint, sinner and child within us. We now know none of these masks can last, and all efforts to maintain the illusion reveals humanity's real goal, the goal of *being-the-being*. Within humanity are all of the forces, powers, and principles of nature. The totality of humanity's efforts, symbolically reflect the creative power within us and is the *god-in-becoming*. Creative abilities that remain dormant in us unfold as the result of our conscious evolution. Our *god-in-becoming* has become the ingrained belief reflected in the world's religions, sciences and philosophies across every tradition of the world.

We must grow out of this self-centered egotistical model of our individualism. Reality is not some imagined or grandiose fantasy that we can barter or plead for. We are the makers and takers of our *being,* and remain free or imprisoned by it. As described by Mircea Eliade in his book *The Sacred and the Profane:*

"Man makes himself, and he only makes himself
completely as he desacralizes himself and the world.
The sacred is the prime obstacle to his freedom. He will
become himself only when he is totally demysticized. He
will not be truly free until he has killed the last god."[19]

This moment is the universe alive within you, everyone and everything. When we redefine god as something less magical, divine or mystical, we unsheathe a double-edged sword. A sword whose blade cannot cut without causing harm to its bearer and we are its bearer, a beautiful or cruel god.

---

19. Mircea Eliade, *The Sacred and the Profane*, trans. Willard Trask (New York: Harcourt, Brace & Co., 1957), p. 203.

The Author

David Sutherland's work has appeared in such quality journals as The Los Angeles Review, The Midwest Quarterly, Oxford University Press and others. David has received a Rhysling Award and a recent nomination for a Pushcart Prize in Poetry. He lives with his family in New York.

Facebook
www.facebook.com/pages/On-Being-The-Being/201905326597899

Website
www.onbeingthebeing.com

About the Type

This book is set in Times New Roman, a font developed in 1931 for *The Times* of London under the leadership of Monotype's typographic consultant, Stanley Morison. The design benefits from a Plantin-like large x-height, and short descenders; it is slightly narrower than Plantin. It is one of the most widely used typefaces in history.

Designed by John Taylor-Convery
Composed at JTC Imagineering, Santa Maria, CA

www.ingramcontent.com/pod-product-compliance
Lightning Source LLC
Chambersburg PA
CBHW052006090426
42741CB00008B/1572